The Last Days of John Keats
and Other Poems,
or
Spoken Histories &
Traveled Landscapes

The Last Days of John Keats
and Other Poems,
or

SPOKEN HISTORIES &
TRAVELED LANDSCAPES

❡ Peter Fabbri Langman

ISBN 978-0-578-00553-9

Published by Peter Fabbri Langman
© 2008 by Peter Fabbri Langman
All rights reserved. Published 2008
Printed in the United States of America

Poems in this volume have appeared in *Crosscurrents:
A Quarterly, Negative Capability, Spirit,* and *Unabridged.*

Typographic design by Joshua Langman

Cover portrait of John Keats by William Hilton, after
Joseph Severn (National Portrait Gallery, London)

This book is set in Arno Pro, a type family
designed by Robert Slimbach in 2007.

Contents

SPOKEN
HISTORIES

The Last Days of John Keats

*As recorded by Joseph Severn, who, when Keats went to Rome to cure
his tuberculosis, accompanied him as nurse and companion. Keats
declined and died at the age of twenty-five, February 23, 1821.*

The surgeon Keats foresaw the poet's death.
He knew the illness all too well, having
Watched mother and brother fall in its grasp.
I do not know if he truly had hope,
Or if the voyage was the last gesture
Of a desperate man; even that went wrong.
We shared a crowded cabin on the ship
With a girl – sick as Keats with the same disease.
Pretty, too, she was, like his dear Fanny,
Still engaged, whom it broke his heart to leave.
His soul went through a multitude of moods;
He'd speak for hours – out of delirium,
Or dream, or brute misery of his plight,
I could not always tell. Most distressing.
Here, then, are his words, as near as I can
Remember through my grief. Forgive me, dear John,
If ever I were less in your kind eyes
Than the honor of our friendship did deserve.

"I thought to call myself a poet, once.
Sad ambition; and now that, too, is gone.
I bid Fame and the Muse, farewell. The chance
Was there. In ill health, things drop one by one,
Till there's nothing left but sickness. Passion
Must find another voice through which to sing;
Mine is silenced. I'm stripped to the bone.
Doctors and impending death clip my wings:
'You must rest; no verse, for the fever it brings.'

They take away my anchor – and my wind;
This sorry ship of flesh will sail no more.
Composing is denied me, but its twin
Brother and opposite steals upon this shore.
The lowliest man who can pull an oar
Stands like a Titan to this feeble frame –
'Hyperion to a satyr.' There is war
Within this flesh; this body once could swim
With vigor in its limbs; now but a decaying form.

Strange, how the thought of dying calls to mind
The memories of flowers. I could see
Myself a daffodil, youthful and blind
To how brief its time. Or, like a daisy,
Sway with the lifting wind, rooted, yet free
To dance in the sun. A primrose – modest,
Unknowing of his worth, but hopeful, if he
Dared to hope. Or quiet, like the twilight
Purple of a violet, awaiting deeper night.

Darkness is descending, and I have done
Nothing. I have knocked upon Apollo's door,
But never entered, standing there alone
Like a boy with a cup, begging. I fear
That all the things I built I built on air,
Magnificent ambitions that were not to be.
The child with the cup had hoped for more.
Is suffering a layer of truth we
All pass through? I long to believe in immortality.

Yes, dear Severn, you may pray for my soul;
And no, I cannot join you in such faith.
But do not fret, for I shall reach the goal
The same as you, and sooner, if the truth
Be told. If doomed to Dover, I shall go forth
To the cliff, and with wide, faithless eyes – leap;
Not go like trusting Gloucester blind to death.
I will not guess at heaven, but will keep
Curious and clear, to greet the path that leads me unto sleep.

Hope, pain, and peace within this heart still clash.
I wish for death each night to end my pain;
At dawn I wish death away, for such harsh
Departure he demands, I choose again
The torment of longing, the unknowing strain,
Nurtured by a perverse hope that will not die,
Despite this evidence of flesh. Who can
Bear oblivion? Give me pain – I'd rather cry
Than cease amid a cloud of doubt, lost in a desolate sky.

The thought of leaving her is beyond all pain.
All night her figure appears and disappears.
The world is shriveled up into my brain
And her pulsing image. I cannot bear
Her vanishings – the lost light – and the fear
Of darkness, of lowering into the earth.
No! Away, foul dream, for I shall endure.
Surrender now would be a certain death.
Her least words haunt me like an utterance of truth.

The woman on the ship – a horrid fate;
Doomed for my journey's length to her dark eyes,
Her skin pale as chalk, like a pearly slate
Whereon death had written. Her drawn face froze
My blood; a childhood phantom that rose
Into flesh; grotesque in youth, and so pale
She compelled my eyes in unbroken gaze,
Watching her gasping and fainting, as frail
As a quivering candle in a dark winter's gale.

Weak she was, but mighty beyond all men
To hold my narrowed soul bound in a cage,
Reduce my breadth of being like obsession
With a lover. Ah, love – the very age
She was of one I love, but on the edge
Of death, this ghostly likeness full of woe.
Paired with this apparition on my voyage
For life, haunted by her I do not know,
Like a vision of sickness from long ago.

And the ship – 'Hark, do you not hear the sea?'
Too well I know its restless, heart-heaved core;
The tumult of its tantrums, and its predatory
Storms, throwing open a harrowing door:
A sinister voice sounds in the waves, a roar
That grasps with cold fingers clamped on my throat,
Lifts my contracted soul and casts it to soar
Through worlds forlorn that mortals have forgot,
As empty as eternal, perilous as the gods' pursuit.

Lost in the waste of the world I had known,
With nothing possessed, but anguish, and the urge
To fulfill all loss and all that's left undone –
Home, love, hopes, desire, plans for the stage –
The fragments torn from me at every age
By death and distance and impending doom.
The ocean haunts me like a troubled sage
Who leads me into hell; but I, consumed
In fear, flee his calling, and fall into my tomb.

Still warm in the grave, overcome in a trance,
I watch a strange parade of shadows pass:
A touch-hungry youth, thrilled with each sense,
Longing to drink up the greenness of grass,
Wrapping his arms round a soft, willing lass –
To find her vanished from his hungry dream,
Alone by a window of darkened glass,
Groping against the pane to clutch a beam
Of moonlight, drunk with its pure, alluring gleam.

Then came a sterner youth, a man obsessed
With seeking in the world his spirit's light;
To find the water that will make him blessed,
And quench his heart's desire. Through the night
He stalks a castle's corridors, his eyes bright
With purpose; searching for his Lady's room
To create a place of lasting delight.
From chamber to chamber he calls her name,
But is lost in a labyrinth, stumbling in gloom.

Followed by one, more desperate in his need;
Once proud perhaps, and worthy of a name,
But long since forgotten. A noble breed
Who pours himself in others and is drained.
His soul was stolen and is gone; the blame
All on a woman. But no peace is there
In his emptiness; only torment – a flame
Burning eternal down a winding stair,
The yearning road to madness through depths of despair.

Then She was there, the goddess cold and wild,
Lover of hungry, searching, nameless men;
The pale mother of a dying child,
Daughter of death, and angel of the insane.
Black was her hair, and gray as ash her skin.
Her dark eyes shone like two wet, polished stones,
Drawing all gazes but giving of none.
Fragile the flesh hanging loose on her bones,
Cold as the moon in a hall of conquered thrones.

Severn! Are you there? Ah, the shadows pass.
What – morning already? I have a sense
Surpassing strange: I see, as through a glass,
My life in England, dismissed by distance;
As if I've died, and all that's happened since
Is but an epilogue acted by a fool
After the crowd has all gone home, his chance
For glory missed. So runs this sorry tale:
A play I did not write, cast in a piteous role.

Where is the fabled song that will not cease?
Who sings of human love that never dies,
Played forever on the sweet pipes of peace?
Is there nothing I can see with these eyes
That will shine as fresh with each sunrise?
Where is the freedom to live as I will,
Clear as the essence of unclouded skies?
How far towards divine can humans fulfill
The wish of creation: to be mighty, and still.

I sought to be a Shakespeare or a Jove:
Creative, receptive, calm at the core;
Steadfast and sovereign – let all others live
In a fever-fit. Well, a rather poor
Performance, I should say. I live with war –
Armies of urges I cannot control.
Where is the peace she promised would restore
Me to myself? Was such a restless soul
Ever crammed into a frame so small?

What knowledge grants Apollo to be god?
What grace can he bestow on dying men?
None, it seems. No salvation for the flawed.
What worth has frenzied striving ever won –
Even if for wisdom, knowledge, heaven –
Still we are here, in youth or age appalled
By death, always grasping for things divine,
Inescapably human, by promises enthralled,
Corrupt in our being's core, creatures fatally flawed.

I'm losing hold, Severn. I cannot last.
The thought of her coils me into a sphere;
All this broad and traveled being is pressed
Into an atom's world – a comet far
Away in space, revolving 'round despair;
And like a comet, burning. All I know
Is her. What I am is nothing more
Than longing for what never was. I can sow
No new seeds; the season is over; nothing more will grow.

I taste death like bitterness on my tongue;
Like the life-blood, displaced, I cannot hold.
I'm a slow explosion outward – the tight-strung
Limbs of a puppet being almost pulled
To breaking; a shapeless, wrung-out cloud,
Fading into mist; all my colors run.
I fear I'll cough myself under the sod –
The earth tastes of decay. Smudging past my bones
And into space – thoughts dissolving – coming undone.

The planet cracks into a thousand parts –
And I am none – centerless – all I feel
Is a queer, circling dizziness – and a heart's
Pulse beating through my brain: the sound of a bell –
Its long vibrations – like some great anvil
Struck – not hammer nor bell am I, but sound –
A rhythm through a mist – I'm but the will
To listen – Severn! The panic; such horror found
In fading. The strangeness is gone; please, wipe my brow.

Severn, my friend, please hear what reason speaks:
Trouble need not be sown, for it will grow
Out of nothing; then why be one who seeks
After anguish? Do me this deed, then, so
Small a thing: the course is plain, we both know
The tale – where's the bottle that I may leave?
A little drink will save us both from woe.
I'm glad there is such a thing as the grave.
Release me from pain, Severn; please, and do not grieve.

What? How dare you deny my chosen end!
He loves me not who stretches on the rack
A tortured and tormented man. No friend
Is this! Cordelia's sorrow could not break
Your heart, nor the madness of old Lear's bleak
And battered love soften your chiseled soul!
You'll string out my days till I cannot speak,
Till only whispers will emerge to hold
You guilty of a broken trust, and leave me unconsoled.

So be it – think not of your suffering friend.
But you, Severn, have you seen death as near
As this? No? Then let me tell you of my end.
Convulsive coughing, coughing and despair;
The wretched throat will choke, the tissue tear,
Gushing up the punished blood blasted loose
From rotting lungs. My very bowels, I fear,
Will reek as foul as when this flesh shall lose
To death, who then begins his maggot-play. Still, you choose."

Again denied, Keats flew into a rage,
Flinging a tea-tray clanging off a chair.
Bitter, disturbed; I did not recognize
The man who spoke; such anger and malice
From obscure corners of his tortured soul.
He stalked the room at a mad, frantic pace,
Wild in his eyes, morbid and pathetic
In his talk – of which, but little I repeat,
For much was more than I could bear to hear.

"Believe your pious righteousness! Prolong
My pain! Is this the kindness of your God?
Grieve for me, for I walk alone in Hell.
Sustain your iron conscience, so concerned
To gain another fine day of life for me.
Fair friend, who torments me and calls it care.
The chain that drags me down to death is more
Despair than disease – a desperate heart
Snared in love – aroused, toyed with, and betrayed to breaking.

And friends – they laughed and scorned my sweetest love.
Dear companions, ever faithful to the far
Ends of the earth; I'd sooner trust Macbeth.
I bared my soul to vultures – foolish man.
Farewell all – parting is such sweet sorrow –
Die with your poisoned tongues stuck in your throats.
You stare, Severn – may not a man express
His mind in words? Oh no! How could I forget?
The kind doctor will hear and bleed me for my sin.

Come, Death – seep into these bones, suck this skin
Pale – is it not my turn? Why not wither
In youth and die? It seems our common doom
To fall before our measured time. Death take
Us all – mother, father, brother – oh, Tom,
I ache with the agony you, too, endured –
A failing love – deceived, deserted, and left
To break – Stop your feeble prayers! I will
Not take a coward's comfort, whatever poison I may drink.

Poison – now there's a naughty word to speak.
What cruel villain could hate enough to kill
This voice – though bitter now, not all unloved?
A fool am I to miss the signs. No, no,
It cannot be. Tom? Are you there? Help me –
I'm with you now, dear brother; do not leave
Again. You died! Cold in my clutching hands,
You died! What madness is death? Do not die
Again. Tom? Severn? Severn – save me from madness."

Then he coughed, and his raving was no more.
The violence of his choking brought him close
To death, reduced him to a heaving mass;
Exploding coughs wracked his frame with spasms,
And broke my heart in his deepest distress,
To see his life's blood spattered on the floor,
With nothing to be done. Hope was a stranger
In that room – cold as ash in our worn hearts,
And forgotten. All we could do was endure.

Thus he was for days – sinking in madness,
Nearly drowning in its turbulent midst,
Rising but briefly to breathe as himself.
Spitting cups of blood – fits of choking,
And fits of fever; he would not last long.
Then, in a trance he lay, skin damp with sweat;
Great mournful eyes staring blank into space.
I knew he could never be Keats again.
I hung my head and wept at his sad passing.

"Severn – wake up. The sun fills up our room
Like a blessing in a sleeping beggar's cup.
Are you shocked by the sun or my sane voice?
The hours of sound and fury you endured
Would bring a Titan to his knees with tears.
The joy of your smile outshines the pouring
Sunlight. Yes, Severn, I am well again.
No, not in body; that I shall never be:
The death-blow has been struck, the echoes fade,

The sound drifts slowly down to silence,
But in that interval I live awhile,
And am whole. Forgive whatever harshness
I have spoken, in this, my darkest journey.
Conceive the words as poisons in a glass
That must be spilled before the glass is clear
And fit to fill with purer wine. I beg
All pardon for this burden, and will hold
Your patient love forever in my heart.

It is you I pity now, dear Severn.
For me, the storm is over, tears are gone;
I let fly all lightning, spoke all thunder.
I feel like clean, clear air after a rain –
So pure it lets light through but catches none –
With winds of sensation breathing through me
That touch, but do not ruffle. I am calm.
But you, having borne so much, must still bear
More, and watch me die. I'm sorry, Severn.

Death is near, but I will not fight nor chase
It now. Indeed, all burning seems consumed.
I move about as in a waking dream;
Not a shadowy world, unreal and vague,
But hard as crystal, more intense than life,
Where day is brighter and the night more black;
And the essence of all things with greater
Force shines upon me, and I, petals wide
To the sun, drink all the glory in. The milk
This morning seemed the sweetest thing I've known.
And how are you, my friend? I sit and speak
Of nothing, while you in silence soothe me
With your calm, abiding presence. Bless you.
Tell me more of daisies in the graveyard.
I like the thought of growing into flowers.
No – no news of friends; I could not bear it.
I'm not as free as metaphor would have me.
Send my remembrance, and if you must tell
Of my ugly journey inward, say also this:
I returned in time to bid them all farewell."

I shall not know again the rich fullness
Of the friendship he inspired. He woke
And cried to be still on earth; the wringing out
Of his last agony. He died in my arms.
Beauty's witness died in beauty. The look
He cast upon me in the end will be
Forever haunting. Farewell, John, poet and friend.

The Cremation of Percy Shelley

As told by Leigh Hunt, who, with Edward Trelawney and Lord Byron, witnessed the exhumation of Shelley's drowned body and its cremation on the beach, August 16, 1822. The passages in quotation marks are Hunt's thoughts as he watched the cremation.

Forty days dead we dug him from the grave;
Coarse sand grains clung to his festering skin.
Ah, the horror of what was once alive –
The rotting face of a prince among men.
He who created glory had lost his soul,
His fearless flight of teeming action done;
A corpse, capable of nothing but its own
Decay – a stinking body in a hole.
That pacing spirit on the run with passion
Was but a lump of carrion and bone.

"The mourner now himself is mourned, but where
Are the shepherds and goddesses?" Instead,
No gods to weep, just we three were there:
Sad, shattered friends who wished he were not dead.
Yes, nature was there, but not as a soul;
The waves of the sea rolled innocently in;
The wind was in our ears, but not to moan.
Still the same – the howling gusts, the cold roll
Of the gray waves that Shelley must have seen –
The sea had killed, and still the sea rolled on.

Like a witness to myth I watched the scene:
The closing down of light that robs the day's
Colors, till all is gray, and nothing known
For real. A torch was lit – the sudden blaze
Turned the evening darker with its harsh light.
In the wind-whipped flickerings of the flame
Pale phantoms played across the sand;
Dim, half-lit shapes like shadows rushed about
And staged their tragic ritual of doom
Like strange, primeval forms of humankind.

What worship for the godless? What prayer
To send an unbeliever to his rest?
If prayer he needs, if rest awaits him anywhere.
I, faithless man, I dream I served as priest:
Like pagans preparing a sacrifice,
We sprinkle oil on his sea-soaked flesh.
I take the flaming torch from Byron's hand –
His dark eyes are wild, his fingers like ice –
My heart increases its tightening clench
As I kneel in the night, and set fire to a friend.

"Good God! How ghastly the yellow flames burn!"
I thought, "Hell is here, and I am in Hell!"
And always the fiery nightmares return,
And always I'm lost in a fiery cell.
Trelawney sobbed, convulsed, dropped to the ground,
His wide eyes in horror, gasping for air.
But Byron wailed like a savage at war,
Charging the sea, and with a wild bound
Plunged into the breakers. I thought with fear
That he, too, was leaving forevermore.

No ghost arose from the sharp-crackling coals;
The fire hissed, the flames blown in the wind
Like a poet's glowing shroud. Circling gulls
Were like pale spirits crying for their kin.
Trelawney, sick with sorrow, was a shattered man,
Huddled on the shore, shaking with despair.
A book fell from Shelley's coat. I recognized
It as the flames curled around and began
Their quick consumption. I even smiled there
To know he had Keats with him when he died.

"If only Keats were here, for he would speak
The language of the gods, and make of grief
A masterpiece to tell the world, and break
The back of sorrow, through beauty, to relief.
If Keats were here – but no! He, too, is dead!
I forget what I knew in this troubled mind.
Shelley penned his elegy a year ago.
He who longed to follow where Keats has led,
To young, immortal fame, perhaps may find
His wish fulfilled. God, that it were not so.

"But Shelley, your Adonais hope is vain,
Unless a nobler realm of souls somewhere
Greets you as a poet worthy of their name.
For I could count the few on earth who care
That you are gone. Who will write – God, not I –
Your Adonais? Who sing your noble heart
In verse? Byron, perhaps, could stand you fast
Against oblivion. Byron – where is he? Why
Did he leave us? Leave us – I hope – no, not
Death again! What – are all our poets cursed?"

I cried until I heard a shout, and turned
To see a creature rising from the waves,
Dark amid the moonlit foam. The fire burned
Like a beacon. He staggered as if the grave
Were calling – fell – then crawled along the sand.
The waves of the flames showed him pale, then dark.
He struggled on his knees, a primitive form
From dim, vast seas emerging onto land.
He heaved his breaths and spit out bitter salt,
Closed his eyes by the fire, and lay down to dream.

Byron. Then Trelawney, mad with grief, dared
Leap up to the fire and with his hand
Plucked from the crumbling skeleton – the heart –
And held it, though his skin was surely burned.
That noble heart – a piece of flesh that's dead.
He saved it as a sacred thing, but I
Want no dismembered relics. Nothing less
Than life will do; the best of Shelley fled
The moment death had come to close his eyes.
Whatever leaves at death is what I bless.

Those last moments – what agony did you endure?
What hopes arose and when did those hopes die?
Were there no hopes at all – the terror pure?
Was thought banished by panic as your cry
Was stifled by the sea? It must have been.
No chance to think or hope or say farewell,
No gentle welcoming of restful death.
Coughing, gasping for air, finding not wind,
But water. Breathing the cold sea until –
The horror – to breathe your last and get no breath.

We gathered the ashes when the fire was done.
The ash was soft like that of any wood.
I could no more hold Shelley in my palm
Than grab some soil and say I held God.
Perhaps he was right, that something unseen
Dwells within us like a heavenly breath.
Regarding his spirit-world of poets, though,
Like Adonais, immortal and divine –
Having been close to poets and to death,
I don't believe it, but wish that it were so.

The Wordsworths' Dilemma

When Basil Montagu offered to let Coleridge live with him,
Wordsworth warned him against it, having experienced the
difficulties of living with Coleridge. Montagu repeated the warning
to Coleridge, who was deeply hurt, and broke off contact with the
Wordsworths. William and his sister Dorothy discuss the situation.

DOROTHY
What is to be done with poor Coleridge?

WILLIAM
The man is to pitied, I suppose,
But for pity's horrible downward stance,
Lowering a severe judgmental rope
To one struggling helplessly below.
An awful thing. No, what he wants is love.

DOROTHY
But love only comes looking eye to eye,
And in those things wherein he surely shines,
He rises like a star above all men;
But where weak, his stature so collapses
He shrinks down to a dwarf's deformity.
He cannot arbitrate his many faces,
Nor hold within his soul a common gaze.
How can another meet him where he is,
When he is truly everywhere at once?

WILLIAM
A pity. With his spirit he could brave
The wrath of Hell to be Satan's savior
And free a fellow-sufferer from pain.
He'd talk the very Devil into faith,
And guide him upward to the brink of grace.
I picture Coleridge with St. Peter at the Gate,
Speaking a soft, fervent flurry of words
To convince the doubting saint all is right,
As saint and Satan gather in embrace.

Not with sham persuasion, but firm faith
In love's redemption. And he'd be right.
He'd do it, too. Just let him plan some more –
Another day's thought to perfect his course;
He'd speak himself into a grand frenzy
Contemplating the wonder of his work,
Be lost in words, and forget all action.
But what a glorious speech it would make.

DOROTHY

Again – what is to be done? Or better,
What can be done? He is an enigma,
A living mystery, a character
Of Shakespeare's, superior to the world,
In one thing deficient: he has no will.
He promises the sun in hopes his vow
Will spur him to action, but overwhelmed
At the task he's set, he freezes, and then
Must lie with tales of further progress,
And so he goes. It's not the opium,
Only; that seems more like symptom than root.
He's a thousand rivaling talents clashing
In disharmony, while the crowd within
Drains his energy without direction;
So lost in his own cloud of suffering
He cannot see the shadow cast on us.

WILLIAM

He is a man both blind and begging, lost
In moral weakness, knowing no restraint,
Helpless to control himself in word or deed
According to his own noble precepts.
How help a man who cannot help himself?
For how long must I receive his abuse –
His lies, accusations, and deceptions –
The trouble that opium brings to a home –
How often must I endure and suffer
For the sake of a friend I still do love?
When does helping become a deepening trap
Preventing him from facing what he's done?
Can it ever be right to turn one's back?
What if that one time is the time he dies?
And yet, he is not all my life – why not

Devote myself to those I hold most dear?
Why does he always look outside himself
For that which can only come from within?
Alas, no magic gives will to a man.

DOROTHY
Weak will is not all – that is but the form
His malady takes. There is much unseen.
One night, hearing labored breathing and groans,
I opened the door to his dark chamber,
Peering in, straining in the candle's glow
To see if he were ill. All disheveled
Was his bed; his face glistened in the light.
He cried out, mumbled, then cried out again,
Sobbing like a child lost in woe. I
Moved not, but felt sweat creep upon my skin.
I seemed a blind man at the Fall of Troy,
Who hears the loud shouts of gods and mortals
In hideous conflict, hears dying moans,
Hears terror-taken breaths, but cannot see
The demon forces battling unto doom.
A blind witness to his nightly torment.
No, William, whatever cause we can name,
We do so blindly. There is some deep struggle
Ever working his soul to ruin, and
All our guessing is but a child's game.

WILLIAM
Then I ask you, now – what is to be done?

DOROTHY
We could talk, but what is talk to him,
Who handles language like a magician
Dazzling a puzzled crowd – what good are words?

WILLIAM
But his is insubstantial dazzling.
People marvel, but walk away no wiser.
Perhaps words grounded on earth, clear and stern,
No room to fly with flashing eloquence –
Confront him with the truth.

DOROTHY
                              But with whose truth?
I fear a lie spoken is a lie believed.
The truth which is to us so plain to see
Is not the truth he knows. I once believed
He knew between reality and lies,
But so consuming are his passions' needs,
I fear the difference dissolves for him.
The worst words he dreads are those which are heard,
Whether spoken or not.

WILLIAM
                              You think him mad?
My God, the man's half-crazy with anguish.
I hurt him. Or Montagu's twisted version
Of my words hurt him. Foolish deed,
To break confidence so indelicately.
Perhaps the foolishness was mine – to speak
Of a man what I would not speak to him.
Where is the honesty in hidden words?

DOROTHY
You cannot blame yourself for another's pain;
You simply followed your own highest thoughts,
Acting with firm belief in what is best.
You cannot count another's unforeseen,
Extreme response as a guilty finger
Pointing at your heart. What more can we do
Than act in accordance with our conscience?
How the world chooses to receive our deeds
Is not our doing.

WILLIAM
                              But I can't remember
What I said, and I fear it was not good.
True, I meant well, but I did not do well.
The fruit of my intention is a bitter
Blossom – a poison spreading between us.
Speaking to prevent harsh feelings between
Friends, I fear I spoke too harshly; perhaps
Frustration spoke resentment or contempt,
Bursting out against all better judgment.
No. I cannot swear my innocence.

This is the truth – there's no denying it.
I have lost a grand and glorious friend.
Exasperating, yes; a nuisance, yes;
A man with eternal troubles – disease,
Nightmares, debts, a severe longing for love –
So deep he seeks the world's admiration;
But a man who leaped into our lives
With the bright vigor of a thriving angel.
Remember how he jumped the fence and rushed
To meet us on that morning long ago?

DOROTHY
I thought we had met with Apollo's son,
This poet new and eager as a fawn
In spring, his animated eyes, his voice
Rolling like a river in its glory.

WILLIAM
I know men who have done some wondrous things,
But Coleridge stands alone of the many I've met
As the only wondrous man I have known.
By some elusive virtue this creature
Is exalted, despite ubiquitous disaster.

DOROTHY
If the friendship is broken, it's his doing.
You offered to meet and work towards healing,
But he refused. Perhaps he needs the break
To blame his failings on another's wrong.
Let him be. You have done enough.

WILLIAM
Is one try enough? Or two? Or three?
What if one more try is all it takes,
But I walk away from a drowning man
Because I tried once and failed to save him?

DOROTHY
But a drowning man reaches out for help,
While Coleridge has run and will not return.
It's not for you to follow where he flees.
And you, though virtuous, are no savior;
Nor is any man. Love, too, has its limits.

WILLIAM
Perhaps. But perhaps I could still do more.
And perhaps I could bear with the burden
That he is a little while longer.
Who knows, that may be all he needs to rise
And be again the giant that he was.

DOROTHY
And if not? Will you forget all others
In quest of a bitter, upsetting friend?

WILLIAM
No, but if virtue bestows peace of mind,
Can this uncertain heart be blameless?

DOROTHY
If you have done ill, it's over and done.
If looking for perfection, you will look
Long, and find only disillusionment.
Even granting your conduct to be flawed
Does not account for Coleridge's complaints.
If you touch a castle wall and the whole
Edifice crumbles into dust, your touch
Is but an inadvertent agent. Is it
Your fault the structure and foundation
Stood precarious? You meant no evil.
He's a misbegotten history of woe;
Even gentle, measured words may well go wrong.

WILLIAM
Ah, but I was not ignorant of how
Precarious he stood. Well have I known
The earthly hell within which he flounders.
He might have been the greatest of our age –
Poet – philosopher – theologian –
If but for fate. Still, what he is, is much.

DOROTHY
I grieve to think the distress his troubles
Bring to others is a woeful fraction
Of the massive heartache he daily must endure.
Yet somehow from storm and cloud he still breaks
Free, shining in a courage all his own.

Perhaps the marvel is he's any more
Than wretched – that he even lives at all.
Listening to his dreams struck me with horror –
A few minutes on a night long ago.
I cannot conceive the weight of his pain;
How joy survives is beyond comprehension.
I see the drooping flesh about his face –
Cheeks grown puffy, body grown large – shot through
With pain and illness so he hardly moves;
His body carried like a mortal burden
He would gladly leave behind. A sudden
Prick upon his spirit's nerves, and all is changed –
Transformed by passion's animating force –
Voice, eyes, face, his whole inspired being
Comes alive with a vast, uncanny call
To listen spellbound as to his Mariner.

WILLIAM

Yes, and when I was down and low in thoughts,
Lost, despondent, wandering in sorrow's fog,
How often Coleridge, and only he,
Would spill forth such a celestial surging
Of words to uplift, comfort and delight,
That I'd see again the spirit's wonder
And joy's dominion, and rise on his wings
To heaven and return to earth restored.
Such is the magic of the man, and all
My words to him are useless to uplift.

DOROTHY

We know he can talk; indeed, all the world
Knows he can talk; but long after his words
Have faded into forgetful silence,
Your written words will continue to uplift.
He'd rather talk and avoid writing's work,
Squandering his genius for a moment's
Short glory of listening admiration.
The solitary, quiet task of art
Is yours, not his, and you shall reach and touch
A thousand unborn hearts for every one
Coleridge descends upon to lecture.

WILLIAM

I would willingly endure his trials
To see him well again, and hear him speak
As first he did when youth made living bright,
And hope flourished blind and abundant; awed
By his rich, astonishing mind, I thought
Here is a poet's wished-for friend. And yes,
He was, awhile, and may be again.
It's hard to bid farewell to one I owe
So much. May time heal what our words cannot,
And bring both friend and friendship to wholeness.

Coleridge Speaks

Coleridge was deeply hurt when Wordsworth revealed
intimate details of Coleridge's life to a mutual acquaintance.
Coleridge refused to see Wordsworth. He is talking to his
old friend, Charles Lamb, about the situation.

That it should come to this – fifteen years of friendship –
No – not mere friendship, but dear devoted fellowship
And communion of the highest kind souls achieve –
For when was I but serviceable and sharing
Of all kindness and the utmost of my being?
To be returned with scorn and bitter calumny –
My God, if vengeance lurked in this gentle soul
He should hear harsh words. "Drunkard! A rotten drunkard!"
"Rotting out my entrails with intemperance!"
Are these words, correctly quoted I assure you,
The sound of sympathy in friendship? No – more like
Betrayal – deliberate – breaking honor's trust,
Spreading a foul contagion of rumored words abroad
Through a man ignoble and ignorant of good.

Wordsworth! Where is the man I joyously embraced?
Your honor, inspiration, and fine, even judgment?
What act is this? What dreadful deed must I have done
To merit whispers of rejection? What foul crimes?
Branded a nuisance and a burden by a friend
To a base, untrusting stranger – 'tis cruel, 'tis cruel.
Granting a partial grain of truth, why violate
The bond and boundary of love? Inviting strange
Invaders to wander through the horror of our home?
Torment enough storms within my skull, I need not
Further storms brewed by gawking, gossiping rabble.
"A nuisance," Lamb! A cruel thing to say, is it not?
More heart-rending still – have I told you all I heard?
They have no hope for me – I am a sunken ship –
I, bitterly needing hope, desperate for their faith,
And they have none. What – am I dead? Can you believe

The resignation of all effort for a friend?
God knows I am no simple guest or easy friend;
Few men have felt their own infirmities as I –
The hauntings of regret are worse than deeds regretted.
But hopeless? A rotten drunkard? True, true, I drink –
Brandy, opium, anything to ease the pain.
Bed-ridden with gout, suffering sore afflictions
Of stomach and back, helpless but for my friends' care –
But hopeless? I did not know unwilling victims
Of distress were abandoned to fate with contempt.

You gaze on a man of many changing faces,
A waning moon where darkness creeps across my countenance,
Leaving but a threatened crescent bright with joy.
Despair ousts all hope from the harbor of my heart,
For like the tides, I cannot be both full and low.
I bear no anger or resentment, but anguish –
Loving them too well to ever cease to do so.
But what I am to do, Charles? What is my course?
I will not crouch to one who brands me a liar.
Reason reminds me forgiveness is a virtue;
My heart cries out against the horror of injustice.
Proud agony forbids meek conciliation.
If love survives, what path does wounded love pursue?

Those who know me little want me ever nearer;
Now those who held me close have sent me far away.
Where is the acceptance that wants me unabridged?
Will no one read this rambling tale from start to finish
Without expurgating dark, unlovely pages?
I am but a ghost of greater expectations,
The shadow of what might have been a mighty man.
To whom I am promised? What must I deliver?
Why is nothing ever enough? What must I do?
I am but what I am – what do they want from me?
I am diversity – a chaos aching to be ordered –
Show me a path, oh Lord, and I will surely walk it.

I see the Creator's doubting face, dejected,
Speaking in a hurting voice, he questions me thus:
What hast thou done, oh noble son?
I have given thee so much, so very much,

What hast thou done with my precious gifts?
Given never less than heaven's withheld key,
Stringent wings for steep ascent to sinless mystery,
Thou hast flapped a circling distance
'Round the multitude of our human truths,
Eyes seeking upward the deep divine within.

This from a dream where all identities are fused.
My dreams are so dreadful, many nights I awake
To a pillow wet with tears, having screamed myself
To consciousness; so disturbing to my loved ones
I nearly become a nuisance in my own home.
The deep divine within – what is divine, but will?
The ability to cause, create, to order
Forth a world, and endow the whole with meaning?
And I, utterly devoid of all volition,
Cringing at broken vows and projects unfulfilled,
Horrified to hear this virtuous voice speak lies,
Driven as a slave in opium's compulsion –
This liberty-annihilating drug that is my doom.

Conversing calms the demons I endure.
To speak, Charles, lifts me out of this battered flesh,
And frees me to a spirit to fly where I will.
For what is flesh, but a needed, coarse appendage;
The vehicle of existence for the mind.
I am not this body, for cut off a finger,
And I am still Coleridge; the finger is not I.
No part, no talent, nor any aspect alone,
Accounts for the magic and the mystery
Of life. God gave the children of Eden power
To choose, and will brought with it evil to the world.
What am I but will – a force beyond the body –
Straining to align itself with the divine,
But paralyzed and shameful, I orbit round God,
The desperate effort suspending me in space,
As inertia keeps me distant with despair.

And so it is in all I aim to do. Whereas Wordsworth
Has his manly way of working to achieve,
Writing with the rising sun's regularity,
I flounder at the chore of setting pen to page.

Such tedious effort is hard upon my nature.
I meant to write hymns to sun, moon, and elements four,
Bringing all opposing forces to reconciliation.
And what have I written of this work? Not a word.
I freeze at the task of contemplated art.
But maybe there are other roads to truth, if not to glory.
Take Beethoven's improvisations, of which I hear
Amazing things – he leaves his listeners weeping with delight.
Now surely none shall hear again those moving notes,
And that, perhaps, will be their lasting magic,
And they will live longed-for and dearer in their listeners' hearts
For coming but once and passing irretrievably to time.
Perhaps, I, too, will be remembered for such moments.

For me a tour for truth is not the destinations
Interspersed with idle tracts of time,
But the richness of the traveling as well;
And no one knows a landscape from a picture.
And if I find a leaf of beauty, I will not
Press it in a book, for always other leaves will come.
Let us look ahead with faith to further glory,
And not hold desperately to beauty dead and gone.

But I cannot even lecture without worry,
Being at my spontaneous best with those I love,
Such as you, abstaining from stultifying judgment.
Safe with the trust and comfort of a worthy friend,
Free to follow and express each sudden whim,
Fearless in the knowledge of your high, abiding honor,
We weave our resonating monuments of sounds.
Self dominates in solitude, petty and perverse,
And builds a fortress to be both prisoner and guard,
Suffering the phantoms of nightmares and madness,
The internal warfare of vast, opposing factions.
But company draws me forth from this foul dungeon,
Administering again the medicine of friendship.
I truly rise and leave behind inharmonious vexations,
Fostered by a sickened state, common and inhospitable,
Wherein the masses of the world live daily and decay:
A thousand vague voices clamoring for peace,
Locked within the skull with no responding cries,
Alone and condemned to only know their echoes.

But I roam into the whole of harmony, a realm
Where intellect and all affective faculties combine,
Guided by imagination's enigmatic leading,
And centered in this instrument of flesh
To sound upon communing souls who gather in its glory.
Books, letters, even poetry itself, all pale
As insubstantial papers, as fossils are to creatures,
Dead matter to energetic life, foreign to the living.
The page is a prison to the freedom of the tongue,
And the spirit's twisting journey through its momentary truths.
Words fixed are words lifeless, predictable and known,
Waiting for a reader to revive their silenced sounds,
Meaning again and again the same unending message,
Reducing all dimensions, mysterious and human,
To black letters on a flat page closed in binding.
Socrates' words were germinating seeds ripe for growing,
Spread with all the fullness of the master's animation.
And Jesus, too, would wander working miracles with words –
Not taking notes nor composing books, but speaking.
These are the ones who writing nothing, are most written of.

Language is the soul's merging and a people's meeting place.
Yet in this merging of the soul, the soul itself's forgotten,
Like the spectrum's varied colors vanishing to white,
To shine a brighter light wherever it may touch –
To become for a second inseparable
From the subject of its shining –
Reality shared in a reach of consciousness,
A greeting verging on embrace and change,
The saving transformations of our troubled lives.
For at this point of being whole, this unitary moment,
All elements aligned as one,
A free and roving will appears and leaves the self
To become whatever it lights upon with interest;
A form of universal sympathy – to be
Equal and one with reverence in all things.
So, yes, it appears I have a will, at least
While talking, though it took me talking to find it.

Yes, it's late, but I fear your leaving me, for dreams
Uncontrolled and horrid claw my weary conscience
Like rats or beasts creeping through dark tunnels
To devour fragile sanity. Please, stay awhile.

Your presence is my refuge, my bridge to better worlds
Than the weird creations rising in my mind.
Without such saving rope I sink into the depths.
What is this torment? Is this affliction a destiny
For waywardness in straying from God's wish?
After Eden innocence is over and undone;
Shrunken love whispers from a severed heart.
Aching heart and grieving head, the crying wings
Of broken wonder soaring from the sun, lost in ruin.
With brightness at our backs we cannot see,
And joy within we cannot find,
We search the world for knowledge and grace,
Blind to our source, and ignorant.

I flee the prison that I am alone.
Perhaps Wordsworth was right – I grasp at love
Too quick to know its certitude or depth,
Fearful to be without welcome havens.
Abandonment is what I always dread,
And now it's come, from one I most revered.
Looking back, it seems all I've ever done
Was done to make me prized in others' eyes,
And prevent such loss as I now endure.
Or else to flee the nightmare world within,
And debilitation of painful flesh.
Such are the spurs with which I must contend.
Or so it seems in melancholy times.
A life, of course, is never so defined,
And I should know that best, knowing my own.

Having spoken truly,
I still could say the opposite
And still be speaking truth.
Driven by what I'm not
To become what now I am,
Or drawn by existence outward
To explore a wondrous world?
Fleeing and preventing pain,
Or pulled by fulfilling joy?
Puzzle out between these possibilities,
And I will call you a clever intellect.
Merge the puzzling pieces into one,
And I shall call you wisest of the wise.

Note, how on this smallest coin the candlelight shines –
Rather like the lunar surface, cold and barren,
Reflecting the perpetual foreign solar gleam,
And like the moon, ignorant of what remote light
Illuminates its world. Which are we, I wonder,
Sun or moon? Are we, with inherent incandescence,
Lights in a dark void, creatures of internal warmth,
The self-glowing center of multitudinous worlds?
Or, like the moon: dull, cold, uninspired bodies,
Reflecting the grander brilliance of the universe,
On one side only, and that through changing phases,
As we roll helpless round a larger, lightless realm,
Like mystified creatures' eyes gazing at the sun?
Say, rather, we are like the flickering candle flame,
Solitary sparks lit by the Creator's fire,
Destined to burn awhile before we lose our light,
Returning to the realm where ghostly fire goes
When thus it fails, and darkness hovers over all.
What? You cannot see the coin's reflected light
From where you sit? Then like the earth's further side,
You are too much in the sun to know the subtle
Glow the moon can give to one inured in darkness.

We perceive the sun as even and eternal –
Like God, a light that shall not perish. Whereas,
The moon is ever-changing like a human life.
But the sun is a fire, and fires all die,
While the moon is a rock and will surely endure.
So much for our finite small perspectives.
Our ever-lasting light is doomed to fail;
Our ever-changing moon is deemed eternal.
And is this not the model of all lives –
How each within contains its opposite,
And none can simply call it black or white,
As with the earth, with darkness over us,
The other side has morning – day and night
Together, as in our souls joy and pain,
Hope and despair, love and anger, salvation
And the forces working against our grace,
Intertwine, and this is life, inseparable,
Rich as a vision from a prophet's eye,
Fascinating as – the time? My God,
Charles, a thousand pardons on my soul!

I can guess the devil's game for me in Hell:
To gaze upon the world and never speak.
Wordsworth said it best I think – bless his soul –
I talk as a bird sings – it's my nature.
Wordsworth – was he not the reason you came?
You see how far I travel once I start –
But then, you know this well. A thousand thanks,
My best and blessed friend. At last, good night.

The Diary of Fanny Brawne

Excerpts from her teenage years, through her engagement to John Keats and his subsequent death, her marriage to Louis Lindo, later days, and beyond.

'Tis a strange thing, this grand game of romance –
The cautious ploys, the strategy in a chat;
Daring and doubt mingling in each sentence
Like uneasy dancing partners just met.
A delight – and a pity. There's no chance
To drop the play and let true love commence.

I'm fond of styles and details of dress.
This is delight. And the mysterious sense
Of meeting a new man – the magic bliss
As sparks fly from eye to eye, full of hints
And hopeful probings to pierce through the dense
Nothing of conversation and pretense.

The pity is the prospect for a man –
Not simply suitable, well-bred, or all
The other qualities a girl can win,
But a man to share my life with. How will
It happen? Will the man I want be gone?
Or what if no one inspires my devotion?

What then? Marry anyway, and hope?
No. Not I. Not without a heart of stone.
That would be a living death with no escape.
But is there any marriage without pain,
And doubt in choosing? And what can atone
For faith misplaced in a wrong-chosen one?

Still, happy couples make their happy choice,
And pledge their hearts forever, and they join
Their lives – but, how do they know? What wise grace
Speaks to them? Is it not a random game
Of luck? Who meets whom? Limited to chance?
Bound by rules of time, place, and circumstance?

And this randomness we base our lives on;
As if once paired, we'll find no other one
Who perhaps may be more pleasing. With all
Our lives to come, we make eternal
Promises to live through things we've never known
With those still new to us and life. Impossible.

∾

Mister John Keats and I have met again.
Beneath his calm courtesy, passions burn.
He feels at fever-pitch: heaven and hell,
Poetry and pain. And what of a girl?
I wonder does he burn for me? I begin
To see love's suddenness – how swift it comes on.

∾

Life was like the sea, with no sight of land,
Clouds hovering low and dark, still without wind.
The future – dim, vacant, pointless, and vast,
A directionless void, shrouded in mist.
Then love rose like the sun, and I was blest –
My vision, my purpose, my course, at last.

For what am I, alone and unloved?
A thing that eats and sleeps, but has not lived.
How potent all emotions now become;
Joy rises at the merest thought of him.
He touched my cheek – I swear my bones dissolved!
My stomach puckered, my breathing heaved.

Life was never empty till love arose,
And all else shrank to trivialities.
Looking back shows me what I could not know –
How empty and aimless was my life's sea.
For love reveals in lifting us so high
The world perceived as through immortal eyes.

∾

Engaged! Dear diary, engaged! Do you hear?
With all the world's women, lovely and rare,
He chooses me. And of all the wise, keen,
And sparkling men this old world may contain,
I've found the one to make it new and fair,
To clean the tarnished stone of love and make it shine.

The knowledge I've questioned at last is clear:
I love and am loved – not vain, simply sure.
Certain to be the center of his dream,
The base that neither time nor passion can consume.
And I shall build with him and all things share,
And weave my world around his sturdy frame.

I could run on the heath, through the long night,
And laugh at all the ageless stars of fate,
Caught in constellations fixed in the sky,
And said to rule with universal sway
Our little lives. Stars, your paths are set –
But we, free as eagles, choose the course we'll fly.

≈

John is still not well, and I, too, grow tired.
I fear his illness deepens, and am scared.
This is not the love I dreamed of. His mind
Is a great antagonizer – bound and chained
With suspicion I cannot understand –
Jealous and bitter – to keep me confined.

He loves me, but I must be his to the full;
He's sorry, but it's beyond his control.
Still he loves me, but is afraid to come –
To see me burns his soul – he stays at home.
My beauty and love have trapped him, he claims.
I pray he awakes from these bitter dreams.

≈

John is so sick, he's moved in with us now.
Mother and I nurse him the best we know,
But with little difference. His spirit is down;
Every seed of trouble is overgrown:
Money, love, mortality; the brute pain
Of facing nothing – a young life too soon undone.

I am salvation to a drowning man;
Love's bond intensified into a chain.
He fears losing me, having lost almost all;
Life and love merge, he sees both turning pale.
If only he'd hear what doubt keeps unknown,
And trust his heart is treasured more than my own.

What once seemed cruel, I can now understand:
His unlovely passion, and words unkind.
I am life to him, such life as he has;
He has closed his hopes around these dark eyes,
And sees naught else. And when he holds my hand,
He holds all he knows of blessedness and peace.

I shall not fail him. He shall know the fierce love
Of angels – devoted, beautiful, and brave.
Whatever harsh word or misplaced deed done
In desperation, compassion will sustain
Him with the patient hands that joy can give
To serve the one with whom I wish to live.

For when calm, he speaks with such eloquence
Of his infinite devotion, Romance
Pales like winter's sun. When he is not well,
Horrible fears consume him, then withdraw.
Thank God, his fits are brief, his love eternal;
For in all things he feels them to the full.

This, then, must be the nature of his soul –
The potent emotions others only feel
In love, he lives with daily as his own.
Meeting him, I met something I'd never seen –
Rapture – sheer delight in great things and small,
The sensitive nerves of intensity distilled.

This, then, is his blessing and his burden –
To travel a path that few have ever gone.
I shall not ever leave him, nor regret
These troubled days, for I have what I have sought:
The nearness to share in each day and night,
To be what I could only be with him alone.

∿

John has gone to Rome in hopes that the warmth
Will restore him to vigorous good health.
But are kind climates enough for a worn
Spirit? I fear what he needs not even
Italy's sweet air, nor ruins, nor myth,
Can give his poor heart. But still, he has gone.

At least he's not alone. His friend, Severn,
A kind and gentle artist, has also gone.
Days are idle; I walk without a word
In the garden, reliving all I did,
And might have done; praying for his safe return;
Lost to all else, wishing he had never gone.

∿

Still no word! Oh, God, why does he not write?
I starve for a word, for just one sweet thought;
But silence – why? 'Tis an ominous sign.
If well, we'd hear. No, there will be no dawn.
And yet – there must – he has a Titan's heart
And a lion's iron will. God, let him return.

∿

His kind soul – noble, destined to be great –
Resigned to die – sunk so low in sorrow's pit –
Tortured till he surrendered to the pain.
Resigned to die – his life did not begin
Without the shadow of its closing coming on,
Death's bell striking midnight an hour after dawn.

I cannot bear the thought of him forlorn
And dying. Please, let it be soft, and soon.
But why was he sent to that foreign shore,
When his friends and I are here with all he knew
As home? I should have sewn us together as one,
And never parted till he was well – or gone.

∾

Dead. A month – and all I can think is – dead.
Charles Brown visited to ease the load.
He seemed surprised to find me not a wreck,
But calm. He did not know a feather's stroke
More of sadness would kill me. "Calm," my God;
Struck nerveless, numb, lost, dissolved. Dead.

∾

All night I walked the heath, till escorted home.
I walked through lonely winding ways of gloom,
Lost in thought, hoping to fall in a hole –
Half-waiting for some violent brute, wild and cruel,
To strike and find me unafraid of doom.
A coward's hope; the courage of a fool.

God! How this hollow body aches to be held,
Enfolded in arms, stroked like a hurt child;
To melt into gentle hands and be fed
On tenderness and never be denied.
I am a pierced heart that once was filled,
Drained by a devouring grief that cannot be healed.

Life is sucked dry down to the bone;
My world is a desert from devotion –
Barren, empty, of all joy forlorn,
And with little hope of its return.
Love's hazard: to be left young and alone.
Waging love against death, love cannot win.

Still, I live. Barely. Pale, thin, sick, and sad.
'Tis strange, but I somehow feel with John dead,
A glory is vanished, an age has passed.
I begin with nothing, where once I was blest.
And his circle of friends – they, too, are lost,
Broken apart, scattered, the harmony fled.

~

Ah, stars – perhaps 'tis well to be so still.
Freedom's blessings are slaves to Time's control,
And subject to every lunatic whim
Of fortune, disease – or a death in Rome.
Circumstance works by no discovered will;
I tried to choose my future; I'll learn – with time.

~

At first I hugged the shadow close to me,
Afraid to let the sorrow slip away.
Agony, like spirit, was sacred and unseen,
Lost to their eyes. Then I tried to lose the pain.
We went to the circus and watched a clown –
I cried that they could laugh with John forever gone.

~

I realize now our pledge was not a choice,
Not the mind's working out to answer "yes."
The earth rose and lifted us to a point
Where stars are friends and breath is heaven-sent.
To deny this would be a soul's death and self-disgrace.
We simply acknowledged truth with our covenant.

There really was no other choice to make;
More like we had been written in Love's book.
Like a flower growing with sun and rain –
They do not choose that violets should be grown.
No. With water and light and all things fine,
It happens. Love is discovered, not chosen.

To be true to ourselves, there was only one path.
We walked it, knowing it would not be smooth,
But that it was ours. This truth was our plan,
And our only guide. We lost it so soon.
Now again I must learn what life is worth,
And prove the love we had was not in vain.

∾

The future, like love, can only be found;
A mystery neither hope nor prayer can command.
So I wander now without hope or doubt –
The curious bemused expression of a cat.
Time is the river I watch with my mind,
Surprised by nothing it carries to my hand.

∾

I woke today in the lap of the sun,
Eager for the morning; but some unknown
Shadow bade me pause – then froze my forgetful blood.
I rose not with tears! Not to mourn! The load
Was gone. Six years of grieving now are done.
I did not wake to death, but life. Thank God.

Today I shed black garments of the grave,
But know, dear John, this means no lack of love.
Grief clothed me in a dark shroud of pain,
But I won't walk in shadow while there's hope for sun.
I cast off all blackness I have worn;
I rise to greet a new and different morn.

∾

There's talk that Louis is too young, or I, too old.
By chance, he's the age I was when John died,
Twelve years ago. What of that? Do not souls
Matter? Age is but a number telling lies.
Hearts know an ageless language without words,
The inner, given voice I trust as guide.

∾

Once again – engaged. Once again, I risk
Losing all, but love's a perilous task.
A heart must breathe, and life is called to live,
Called by a voice deep in the soul. I have
Found a sober joy, a soft happiness;
Hope is returned, but not without distress.

Ecstasy is muted in me this time,
But I think lesser love is not to blame.
I will not spread myself on the wings of delight
With youthful abandon. 'Tis my past fate
Holding in the reins to keep me safe and sane.
For love, once crushed, is wiser in its dreams.

≈

Motherhood is come, a rich and trying time.
Birth is the miracle of life brought home
To shine in weary and distracted eyes,
Renewing wonder with this life who grows
With love. 'Tis love made flesh, as is life's aim,
Creation weaving through our earthly days.

≈

Love's underside is long hardship and work;
Daily duties hide love in the indifferent dark.
Human lives clash like tangled, tender nerves;
Hearts that lose passion, then patience, will starve
If love's forgotten. Like all things alive,
Love must be well-nourished to survive.

≈

Dear diary, this young girl is now turning gray.
My old family, of course, was gone long ago.
But the young ones, too, are grown – gone to where
Their lives have led. And I have little more
Ahead. Love leaves me with grateful hunger –
Filled beyond hope, needing love forever.

≈

The postscript: after death her spirit speaks.

Though wife, mother, and spirit, I still dream
Of John – the quiet garden of Wentworth Place;
Walking hand in hand in summer on the heath,
Tingling as his eyes flashed into mine.
How bright the sun was, and how cool the shade.
Flowers were fair fantasies of colors,
Sprouting from shy, luxurious deep green.
The plum-tree nightingale singing rich songs –
Fulfillingly elusive of completeness,
A delightful fate never quite arriving
With its promise, but sweet with expectation.
Birds, flowers, sunlight, the wind on the grass –
The thousand little things that he made live.
It seems a separate life, a magic time,
The Eden we all dream of deep inside,
But never know. I wonder if it was.
I still wake from these dreams with a hollow,
Aching heart, and this, a lifetime later.
And Brown, too, twenty years after the death,
Sorting through John's papers felt such deep pangs,
And sensed John's presence watching like a ghost –
So vital and alive he was in life –
Brown's nerves trembled with pain and remembrance,
Worried to do justice to this young man
Who bravely lived life's vividness till death;
Sobbing overwhelmed him. And Brown, a sturdy man.

There's no one alive who ever met John;
My God, how history rolls, relentless and swift.
And so, I, too, shall be all but unknown;
My children will live but a little while,
And be forgotten. Such brief appearance –
Filled with dearest pathways long untraveled,
And countless questionings of fate, pointless
And inevitable. All is unforeseen. And yet,
I sometimes had a sense when things were right,
Of how to be the best that earth allows.

But the gifts we're given are so quickly gone;
Time disperses people, keepsakes, and their tales.
Severn in Rome – a young, rising artist –
Remembered not for his life's work painting,
But as a loyal friend. Brown – dead in New Zealand,
Lost to the world in a forgotten grave,
Remembered as a friend. So are we all,
Footnotes to a greater name. Such is Time,
Who withers the tree but preserves a leaf.
All things dwindle – books and rings and letters
Get passed along to those who know them not,
Lose their meaning, and slowly drop from sight.
The house we lived in was to be torn down;
But John's name, like a melody unheard,
Played urgently on distant hearts
Who gathered in the magic of his calling.
His saving legacy preserved our house,
Drew from distant hands gifts and treasures
Passed along a hundred years, and brought them home.
The force of who he was has countered Time,
Pulled from oblivion a thousand scattered things,
To hold their story hallowed by his name.

He played the strings of innocence and joy
When hope was dark and sorrow strong.
Peace, perhaps, he never knew; but grace,
Though shadowed by his agony and grief,
Found in his heart a welcome home, and did abide.
Innocent, eager, earnest, and wise –
The beauty of his being is a song
Rousing the heart to find its own true voice,
And sing. This, John, is the genius of your love,
And you, its great presider. Sleep well.

Lord Byron Leaves England

When Byron's wife, Annabella, left him early in 1816, no reason
for the separation was made public. Rumors spread regarding
Byron's alleged incestuous relationship with his half-sister Augusta,
and of his alleged homosexuality. At that time, homosexuals
lived in fear of mobs and capital punishment. Byron is reflecting
on his life on his last night in England, April 24, 1816.

I leave you, England, like a brave Adam
Freed from Eden – gone gladly and for good.
The binding confines of your little land
I leave behind. Even the ties of blood
Cannot keep me. I am a swinging blade
Severing the chains of this fog-infested shore;
The cold, brooding bleakness of this land of prudes
And barbarous laws shall haunt me no more.

I shall go again to Greece, where the sun
Shines naked in the sky; where passion has no shame;
Where the great gods loved when sin
Was not a shadow to darken passion's flame.
I have still a world before me, and dreams
Of destiny that will not be forgotten.
This will be no exile – I banish them
To live in darkness, while fate calls me forth – lead on!

And so I go, and all because of love;
Because lost amid the laws and statutes
Of the land, affection cannot live.
And the transgressor reaps the bitter fruit
Of daring to stand alone. How remote
A loneliness it is, none else can know.
Who dares defy the times? Who casts his vote
For the damned? Who stands by me? Precious few.

And what is love that stirs so strong a storm?
The magic that makes every man a fool
Fit for a stay in Bedlam. The form
Of madness varies, but never the rule:
All succumb to idiocy – a real
Spectacle in those who do it well;
Though some suppress the foolishness, and deal
Only in the strictest lust. In both, I excel.

Why, well before I knew what sex was for,
(Though sometimes still I wonder even now)
I cherished faces that I still adore,
Even those the law does not allow.
Such was my hunger, anyone would do,
If only beauty dwelt within their eyes.
I worshipped faces that I scarcely knew,
An apostle whose only prayers were sighs.

I sought salvation in the wedded state,
In legal lust and lawful pleasure;
I needed a mooring to keep me safe
From dangerous wanderings. But no harbor
Holds the ardent soul, and it was torture
To be caged with logic's little princess.
Her calculations could not comprehend the measure
Of my wings – nor the depths of my hidden emptiness.

She was to be my angel of mercy –
To keep my ship from being wrecked.
(I might have done better with Lady Jersey,
But she, too, is a hen, and her husband looks pecked.)
I propose a practice marriage, to detect
How much each can accommodate:
How much the woman sees to correct,
And how much the man can tolerate.

I thought a settled life was what I wanted –
A peaceful home and quietness to write.
But it seemed like I was being hunted,
Or followed by God's interfering light.
The peace was boring – I had to take flight;
But she hung on me like a deathless harrier –
Attentive, and appallingly polite.
You may admire a saint, but do not marry her.

Poor Annabella, bound to such a beast
As I – how could you even think to love
This melancholy scandal? True, at my best
I laughed and sang and clowned and was alive –
Though usually not in ways you would approve.
And joy, it seems, was not your strongest suit.
In morals you excelled, but could not save
Your husband, thus proving I was a hopeless brute.

I am an outcast in an English world
That prides itself as culture's prize –
Civil and sane and correctly moraled.
They watch with primitive, punitive eyes
For deviation from their narrow ways,
And pounce with murderous intent
On one who threatens or defies
Civility's model they represent.

What ghastly horror am I guilty of?
Assassination? Treason? Murder?
Rape? No. But they'll kill a man for love.
Who has been harmed? This they cannot answer.
What have I done but follow love's nature
As it manifests in me? God, I could kill
A man and be less a social danger
Than love one, and go to the gallows as a criminal.

All my vices have been the lawful ones
Of lust and romance, or the unlawful
But accepted sins of fornication
And adultery. But these are quite dull
And commonplace, and the world pays little
Heed, unless the players have sufficient fame,
And even then they are not criminal,
But merely gossiped of, and more with envy than with blame.

But my "criminal" contacts have been pure
Beyond the fleeting lust of flocking birds
Who danced before me. God, to have a whore
Is smiled upon; but to love beyond words
A sister – or a friend – when the guards
Of goodness are against you, is a fate
Not to be envied. Even Shakespeare's ill-starred
Lovers were spared the idiot mob's hellish hate.

For I have reveled in an ancient crime,
And found solace in forbidden flesh,
And would again. And why not? I could roam
The world for women and watch beauties flash
Before my eyes, and find nothing to match
The tenderness I've known. Ah, but the laws,
Always there are laws, but laws should catch
Criminals, not condemn affection in private halls.

Love is our deity – all seek true love;
I cannot count the bodies I've been through.
Then once I find it, I am forced to leave
The country. Where else find a heart so true
As in a sister? Who else could know
Me like none other? Who else take despair
And ease it? Make me laugh when I am low?
And love with less desire than ever-deepening care?

Where all my sins are known, and forgiven;
Where all my moods come safely for release;
Where my faults can find a graceful haven;
And where the shipwreck of my heart finds peace.
If this be love that wears so kind a face,
Then once I found it – once, and never more;
The only love I never had to chase,
The only soul to make my spirit soar.

Incest! A hideous word and hateful to hear.
Unnatural act, vulgar crime, vicious sin –
Such lovely terms for love. And yet I fear
It is my fate – our fate – for we are twin
Inheritors of a dark ancestral line.
For to be born a Byron is a thing
Most strange – for as the world looks we seem to shine;
But behind the bright curtain, tragedy is king.

I picture God upon the moon, amid
Myriad worlds, and space as vast as time,
Casting imponderable eyes 'cross the void
Of planets, stars, and comets full of flame.
And I wonder if somehow in this scheme,
As an atom in the cosmos, God cares
Who I touch, and how. Whatever became
Of privacy? I wish He would keep to His own affairs.

And if God be but a dream of men,
And commandments but a culture's code
For order, to bind with prohibition
Nature's urges – then why follow such a crude
Contrivance? Why not run free and be true
To something other than man's moral invention?
Besides, the code is old and should be reviewed;
It's time the moralists called a new convention.

For countless are those who privately sin;
And though they do not count it sin, they dare
Not risk the madness of the mob, and in
The dark, behind the public faces of their
Lives, carry on with constant threat and fear.
In brave obscurity, they practice what
Is never preached; they are like clouded stars
That cannot be seen, but burn somewhere bright.

And yet, if these were the great days of Greece,
Or if we followed in Turkey's footsteps;
Or for the other of my calamities,
If I were Pharaoh in ancient Egypt,
Where they wed within families, to keep
Pure the royal blood, then all would be well.
But the Byron doom placed me where I must escape,
And the Christian doom will place me in Hell.

Why do I feel as if my life is done?
I'm eight and twenty – to the world a youth –
But my sense is of declining days. Gone
Are hope and expectations, and the earth
Is but a place I've been before, with
Nothing more to do. I feel like a void –
An urn filled again and again with mirth –
That is cracked and hollow and nothing more can hold.

I've been too deep in decadence, too long.
I was initiated by a maid
When I was but a child. Perhaps a wrong
Was done – I do not know. But something died
Within when she came into my bed;
And something else was born – an impassioned search
For something like a god – a human god
Of innocence whose spirit mine could touch.

I am sick of vice. The endless nightmare
Of delinquencies has haunted me too long.
So many bodies – for some I did care –
But most – appetite and intrigue, nothing
More. What a gay parade of ghosts comes calling –
To grin and gloat. I cringe at the indulgent waste
I fondly call my life – a sterile string
Of birthless copulations by yours truly, "Lord Beast."

Sensual indulgence was once my life –
Now it seems like death; and yet we are made
For this in body – we are all the proof
Of God's intention that we mate and breed.
But Lord, are we only bearers of seed?
Have we not mind or soul or something more?
Are we not like a diamond lost in mud?
Who seek for an angel, but settle for a whore?

Virtue I need, for vice is emptiness –
A moment's pleasures are in a moment
Gone. But what is a man to do – confess
And be a monk? Not without a convent
Near. A monk – now that would cause some wonderment
In London – they'll talk of it on every block.
I'll announce I've taken the sacraments –
Who knows, perhaps my wife will die of shock.

Perhaps there is an element perverse
In the dungeon of my deepest urges;
An atom out of place; a kink or curse
Within the wrinkles of my brain; a drunken judge
Who bids me act on the eternal stage
One play only – and so again and again,
Like an unlearning imbecile in a cage
He cannot see, I bring all the Furies down.

For what I seek, I get – and then repent.
And yet I seek again. I have a thirst
Not always wise. Perhaps at times I went
Too far; perhaps some things are simply cursed,
And sin remains sin from first to last.
Perhaps. But why does a voice within cry out
Against this? Is it blindness, or the clearest
Sight of all? Annabella could tell me, no doubt.

My life is closing as I fill with guilt.
I am a seed that could have been a rose,
But chose not to blossom, only to wilt.
And God, the road to dissolution goes
On and on, and I follow as if in a daze.
But then, to our talent we must be true,
And my pathetic genius is to find new ways
To be a prodigy of decrepitude.

Age is an awful thing for youth to bear.
I thought there was a sequence to the years
Between manhood and the grave. But I wear
Too soon the signs of Time, and the grave nears
When it should still be distant, and it scares
Me when even Time cannot be trusted.
Perhaps like a race run too quickly, my share
Of living is done; and though bright while it lasted,

I would that it were not yet over.
I feel betrayed by Time, but I suppose
My deeds are my doing, and as a lover
The lines were long and I was willing. But those
Pleasures have their vengeance. My body shows
The wounds like a soldier back from decadent war;
Aged from the ravages of dangerous applause,
From drink and indulgence and the clap from a whore.

The mirror tells the story of my life –
The corpulence, and puffy bloat of age;
Hair turning gray (I'll blame that on my wife);
Even my teeth – how can the lion rage
Whose teeth are loose? I'll send for my carriage
To ride into Hades, for death's canker
(With great assistance from my marriage)
Is spreading fast. I must write my wife and thank her.

Ah, but I am not well; something is amiss;
For there are footsteps in the hall at night,
That are not there. And always the darkness
Is a fearful thing, as if there might
Be something. My God, have I been mad? What
Could there be? Nothing, and yet I have paced
With loaded pistols, expecting to shoot,
As if I were stalked by a merciless ghost.

Newstead was haunted, people used to say;
I heard all the stories when I was young.
But there are footsteps even when away –
As if I were followed – as if the thing
Were after me – or in me – like a walking
Premonition of some doom, or a dread
Messenger come with words beyond hearing.
I wait – dagger in hand – till the footsteps fade.

There are dark things in the world we do not know;
Unearthly things we cannot give a name;
Sensings of the soul, that like a cloud, flow
Through awareness, and agitate the brain.
What is the soul? And what the source of dreams?
And sleep – why must creatures close their eyes –
And at night – when things the daylight tames
In other realms, awake from sleep, and rise.

Perhaps this path leads to enchanting things –
To deeper truth of God – to where all souls atone;
But the world of night and imaginings,
Of dreams and tales half-told; of ghosts and bones
And wicked things – against all rule of reason
I am prey to morbid thoughts and invisible
Influences. Of course, I've always been a pagan
At heart. But I do not sleep without my pistol.

But there is little of peace in my wild sleep;
And dreams – my dreams, Augusta, I don't dare
Reveal, for they are things I would escape.
Though in life you have been my prayer
Answered – in dreams you are no longer fair,
But rise up like a demon to attack –
Terror closes my throat, and the nightmare
Leaves muscles tight and skin wet; I shiver when I wake.

If thoughts and dreams can make my being quake;
If flesh is moved by what it cannot touch;
Perhaps we should bow to unseen things, to break
The bars of this our sensual cage.
Is thus the body but a little bridge
To reach from soul to soul across the void?
To be the instrument and voice of each –
The performer, not the poet; the body, not the bride?

If the soul – as in my nightmare's ravages
Upon my heart and breath, sinews and skin –
Rules the body's realms like appendages
To its divine command, is spirit then
Primary over matter? Are all our cells peons
To the soul? In dreams, at least, it so appears.
And in love? Will not a lonely soul, a broken
Heart, bring ruin, weakness, and relentless tears?

Is the foundation of the world not earth and stone,
But spirit? Can it be? Well, flesh decays –
Of this I am daily reminded by one
Look in my mirror; but soul – are its days
Numbered? You know, I half-believe death frees
Us forever. Half is a fair estimation –
I may even raise it a few degrees
When I know my eternal accommodation.

Of course, biology has its revenge –
A bullet in a bone affects the soul,
For fleshly pain will give the mind a twinge
Or two. And wine will help release control
From a too-tightly ruling spirit. The real
Question to be answered by our sages,
Is – which rules in lust and love: flesh or soul?
I'd answer, but it would take too many pages.

What purpose flesh? If I were God and made
A soul, would I enclose it in so poor
A house, a being so brief? I would trade
This flawed and fatal flesh for a life more
Light than laden, more like a breath of air
Than encumbered bone. Ah, though touch is sweet
And intimate, its lust and luster wear
With age, as if a flame could lose its heat.

Love is the literary masquerade
Of flesh – the bright veneer we put on beasts.
We think, in our cleverness, we choose to mate,
And dress it up with lace and sentiment;
But like all species we are pulled, puppets
In an old parade, moved by strings we cannot
See, and in our folly we decorate
An act we cannot understand, and yet repeat.

But if this is the tune of the world's great waltz –
Then what am I? To what mysterious strings
Do I dance? Perhaps the puppet-master lost
His place, or lost his mind – who knows? These things
Happen, I suppose, to beggars and kings,
And of course they happen to me, yours truly.
Maybe I'm running free with broken strings –
A frightening thought. No wonder I'm unruly.

I should have been an orphan. My father
Was a name to me, and not a good one.
My mother – she bore me, though I'd rather
She hadn't. And I had an orphan's
Dreams of idols that came crashing down;
And hopes for a magic destiny, with gods
And goddesses around me. And yet within,
I seemed a thing deformed, doomed to solitude.

And there is matter's insidious rule –
An ill-formed foot on an innocent boy.
What subtle havoc in the realm of the soul
A flawed foot can wreak. What a life – to be
Poor, tormented, and alone, with little joy –
Then wealthy, known, and social in a day;
I was the god that others dreamed of, as I
Had dreamed; but this god's feet were worse than clay.

Then the wave of fortune broke, and again
I am alone. They caught glimpses of the god
Within, and saw too dangerous a pagan
To endure my presence. By my own deeds
I am adrift, or by my accursed
Nature, which seems beyond my foot or soul,
And was made by a creator wild or mad,
As if I were destined to create my own Hell.

Of all things in religion, damnation
I believe, for I have been outcast and damned,
And felt for years the shadow of my sin
And separateness, as one not made for man,
But a destiny apart I can't define.
Though this world is all we know, with no escape
But death and its questionable release, I've seen
Enough to welcome, without risk, eternal sleep.

For what salvation do the damned deserve?
My soul is stained, and not my soul alone.
This fact remains; forgetless Time preserves
All deeds. The clock of years cannot return
To days of innocence, and acts are not undone
By pious words and desperate prayers. Guilt must
Be borne as a burden of stone, or a poison
To be swallowed for the soul to digest.

The fault was mine, Augusta – you are free
Of blame; but I have cast on your character
A blot undeserved that belongs to me.
If only Annabella's first answer
Were "yes." But between her first refusal and our
Marriage – in those two years with you of bliss
And horror – we did what we can never
Speak, though even now I long for your caress.

And such is the strangeness of human touch,
That your caress is like none other.
Yet, skin to skin, is it not the same? Does flesh
Distinguish compassion from desire?
It must be spirit and skin together
That make love's caress the pinnacle:
Where the soul exalts the earthly,
And the senses enrich the soul.

And so I bid farewell, not to England,
But to you. After you, what love I find
Can at best be pale. And if we have sinned,
At least it was out of a love so blind
We forgot the world and left its ways behind.
Not hate, nor malice, nor ambitious greed
Were ours; we were but two souls in kind
Who found the answer to our deepest need.

May you be untroubled by the darkness
I brought, and may your days be bright and full
Of joy. And I? I go to find a place
That welcomes sinners – preferably not Hell;
Though if options are few, I might as well
Join all the world's best company.
Even Jesus went there once, I heard tell,
But had reservations elsewhere, and could not stay.

Perhaps my carnal candle has gone out,
From England's dampness or too much burning.
I hope to rekindle it in the South,
Where lovely ladies do their yearning.
And once I'm gone, I'll not be returning
To this quaint little island I leave behind.
I've learned that for the heart's great burning
Other countries are more erotically inclined.

Not much of a lesson for years of study,
But then learning is not my best pursuit.
My rivers of thought tend to run muddy
From lust and liquor and all sins of repute.
But having said this, I am not a brute,
Though my wife and others share this opinion –
I wish I could give them all the boot
And send them down to the devil's dominion.

Coleridge: Out of the Maelstrom

1 Coleridge, alone in his room with Charles Lamb.

"Failure, like the closing of a coffin-lid,
Is come upon me. I have murdered
All that was holy and wise within this frame,
Banished from all better days to roam
Like a ghost condemned to watch in horror a knave
It suffers with but cannot act to save.
I cannot speak tonight, Charles. I cannot speak.
Announce the lecture's off – tell them I'm sick,
It's true enough. Do you know what it is to perceive
The death of all one has that's worthy to live?
Death, Charles, how death haunts about my darkest dreams.
God, to sink to the stillness of stone seems
An envious fate; or to sleep a million years
And wake to know I'd sleep a million more.

What is the matter? My God, Charles, what is not?
What sphere of this bitter farce still shines bright?
Have I not wrecked all? Name them – father, husband, friend;
Poet, publisher – lecturer; and damned
By all as lazy, lying, immoral and weak.
Jeered and scolded as if for pleasure's sake
I chose degradation; as if I chose this hell.
'Let him choose differently,' they say, 'and all
Will be well.' Go bid a blind man open his eyes
And gaze upon the world; he need but choose.

No, I cannot go tonight. Every judging eye
Is on me, ready with a laugh to say
They've heard it all before but now they see it's true –
'He really is a wreck.' I cannot go.
And Wordsworth is in town – no doubt he'll come
In triumph and to justify his whim
Of making gossip of a friend by proving
It's all true. He'll gloat instead of grieving
For one who looked to him with honor in his eyes.
I will not face his condescending gaze.

There is more to tell – after the lecture last week
A woman introduced herself – we spoke,
And met for dinner the next day. It was a friend –
An old friend – Mary – my Mary – the hand
That I first longed to hold – the first I longed to wed –
Long married now as I am, and as bad
A match. No – far worse – a disaster of a pair.
Both married in misery because fear
Prevented me from speaking what was in this heart.
God, is it not the cruelest of the hurt
That this grand mouth that cannot ever seem to cease
Should fail utterly and bring us such loss.
A cruel fate; I cried all night for what might have been,
The bliss that might have kept me as a man.

I had Mary's love once; I had Wordsworth's, too.
I had esteem from many – even me.
But where is love when dignity is dead? All gone.
What is left for me but to be a stone,
To find the sleep that endeth not? Can it be wrong?
No, suicide is not a blessed thing,
But perhaps it has its place. Please, do not stare,
The room was checked last night and is now clear;
The fit was on me then, you see, but not for long.
Which is worse – continual degrading
Of what once was fine, suffering in body and soul,
Agony and shame, helpless and feeble –
Or to make a stand with courage as a final bow,
Bid a firm, dignified farewell – and go?
If only the wish could carry the act by mere
Intent, and the spirit's will deliver
What else remains undone. Opium is a maelstrom –
The deeper I descend into the storm,
The more I see the danger; but the more I further go,
The more I'm pulled – there's nothing I can do
But die – by my own hand, or by opium's slow,
Tortuous crawl towards death. There's no way through
The mire – like quicksand – each struggle to escape
Drags one deeper. No. I have no hope.
A hundred times I've tried to walk away, to free
Myself, and a hundred times again I
Cringe, convulse, even scream with agony, and cry

Like a newborn child, driven every day
To drink from the bottle of promised doom. With enough
Money I could give my dear family half
And place myself in a madhouse for proper care –
But there's no hope being alone and poor."

Coleridge screamed and fell with trembling to the floor.
Lamb jumped up, started, then froze with fear,
Watching his dear friend writhing like a wounded worm,
Gasping as if drowning, and then a scream.
"The bottle from the book-case – give it to me – quick!"
He drank, shuddered, and stretched out on his back.
Then slowly, he raised himself and sat on his bed.
"You see how it is – I cannot be mad
For contemplating death. Anyone else would do
The same. Even the best of men must know
The battle's end, when the last of enduring lights fail.
Charles! Be not so harsh with me until
You know what it is to live in this flesh and soul.
Damn it, man! Plague me no more! Or I will
Sting you in return. I'm not rotting carrion
To be picked at by scavengers for fun!

You poke me, and I feel small stirrings within;
Not dead, but weak; not helpless, but worn;
So used to paralysis it became assumed,
Not proven, and I the willing victim.
Perhaps I have been weak; perhaps I can do more
In brave resistance. I shall wage a war
One final time. The backward look is bleak
And full of shame enough to make me sick.
This cannot be the life that I am meant to live.
I cannot let their mockeries thrive.
A growing sense of debt to my own buried soul
Strengthens me to strive again to be well.
I have suffered gross injustices to my honor.
If nothing else I do, I will never
Rest until I beat down the bitter calumnies
With truth as my witness. I must make peace
Between the self I am and far too long have been,
And the Self that cannot cease to be. Well then,
Leave me to prepare. I will speak tonight – but please,
Promise you'll attend. Thank you, and God bless."

Coleridge enters the lecture hall late, hurried, out of breath; disheveled, glassy-eyed, and a bit disoriented.

"Forgive me, dear friends. Welcome, and thank you. Let us begin.
The theme tonight – the theme – yes, a play of Shakespeare's – the
    theme
Is love. Or is it passion – the play of passion – the play
Of Shakespeare's – from Bandello of Italy and Brooke
In England, with fourth-century Ephesian derivation
In elementals of plot, but given its final form
By Shakespeare, known today as 'Romeo and Juliet.'
Now Chaucer's Prioress would have us think 'Love Conquers All,'
But here the greatest lovers die a violent death
By virtue of love invincible and devotion blind.
And this is love unquestionable – is it not? Or is it
Passion, perhaps, or madness – the taking of youthful lives
Is rarely labeled sane. And yet, can suicide be sane?
Perhaps. And madness by its meaning cannot be called sane,
But can it be rational and self-murder justified?
Brutus, Cassius, Antony, Cleopatra, Othello –
All chose suicide – no faint hearts, these, but a noble lot.
Willing to forego all future to end present torment,
Or prevent a future, feared occurrence – to be jeered at,
Laughed, scorned, mocked with dignity's derision, the utter shame
Of being less than human, less than they were, the dreadful
Drop from nobility to baseness. For this our dear friends
Chose death – no, not as cowards, for who cannot conceive
Their plight? Threatened with being specimens for show
To vulgar, callous crowds; stripped of dignity in friendship
And love's illimitable comfort; turned from gods to goat-herds,
Inglorious and scorned; a hero's metamorphosis
From magnificence to fool; prisoners of loathsome pain,
Conscious as Prometheus in torment, and as helpless;
Faith starved by suffering's wasting purge; and still they found
Salvation's darker door. Bravo, I say, for they stood firm,
Refusing an inhuman martyrdom, daring the unknown,
For what is death that we should fear it so? Who can tell me
Why we shrink from mystery to bind ourselves to torment?
Only madmen suffer needlessly when a path is clear
To freedom. Madness, then, is to stay hopelessly alive,
Against all chance of gaining even an hour's peace from pain.
Romeo, rather than walk through Hell's devastated halls,
Alone, assaulted by agonized longing, ripped of love,

Forever walking with she who will never walk again,
Grief-blasted, spirit-wasted, shorn of his world – is this life?
What further depth could death reveal?
                                        And yet, poor Romeo,
Your act caused calamity greater than love's damnation
Of eternal separateness of wedded hearts; die again
A hundred times, suffering soul, for the outcome of your deed.
Your chosen course brought your one beloved a needless death.
The blade pierced her heart because you died, because you were weak
To endure your grief another day, another hour –
Where was your strength to stand and honor by enduring all?
Seeking to escape a pained and noble grieving, you fled;
Fearful to bear a worthy sorrow patient in your heart,
To outlast agony instead of cheating honest grief
By ducking to oblivion to miss the rage of pain.
What haste unholy stole upon you, what rush thus murdered
Your morning on earth of its fairest light and fondest love?
Hurrying fool! Your beloved lived! On the brink of bliss
You stood and knew it not, too sure the future was all slain.
Fool! Fool! Think of the joy unparalleled, the utter joy,
The wonder worth waiting a thousand, thousand years to know,
If you had but patience, and as you kissed the pale, cool lips,
Her breath stirred, her eyes opened, and gazing in a moment
Known only to gods, you watched your love awake from death
And rise again to life, holding her reviving body
Heart against heart; hope and despair in dazzling confusion;
Laughing tears of woe transformed by the pristine ecstasy of dreams,
And in transcendent seconds, blood and breath surging, spirit high
      and spiraling,
To take her hand, still dazed, and walk out of a tomb to paradise.
And these are but moments; think what years unseen of love were
      killed.

If Romeo could speak, perhaps he'd say:
'Be wiser, all Romeos in the flesh;
Look not for love beyond the gates of death,
For visions come, awful and clear: mother
And father in horror at my grave;
Despair cast on the fairest friends on earth;
But worst, condemned in helplessness I watch
The knife's plunging into Juliet's heart,
Feeling every screaming nerve cry murder
In dishonored ears; wretched, powerless

To act. This is the very depth of hell,
Awareness without will, incapable,
A shadow sharing only in despair.'

Too late he learned even the wise foresee not the future.
Therefore, shut not your heart when darkness comes, but bind your
    souls
A thousand times tighter to multitudes of joy. Welcome, then,
The friends forgotten, the love unlooked-for, new wonders to see,
And old ones, too, that never lose their curious magic:
The unreachable mystery of children and their ways;
The soul, after tumultuous storms, rising to wholeness;
Little blessings we cannot name, that are too close to know,
As are the elements of health, and mine being poor tonight,
Summon me now to close and seek a most elusive peace,
For wellness dwells with hope and nourishing, and after effort,
Rest is heaven, and I shall sleep tonight more easily,
Restored by my own outpouring and the honor of your interest,
Which gives so much in quietness. Thank you. And remember,
Let us again be grateful for the source that gives us hope.
Misery breeds, but hearts endure; thus let us try, and peace,
Perhaps, may come at last, and with it love or kindliness.
Aim for all good things in the spirit of sustaining love,
For though sorrows come upon us, I trust the clouds will clear.
Hold fast to spirited flesh, my friends; trust in strength untried;
And I will speak again, as scheduled, on the suffering of Lear."

Southey Meets Shelley

Robert Southey was an early supporter of the French Revolution and
a political activist. He and Coleridge planned a Utopian community
in America, but this never materialized. Southey's radicalism
faded and his domestic duties involved him at home. He has just
met Shelley, who is full of revolutionary and Utopian schemes.

Can I be so old at thirty-seven
To meet the ghost of my own youthful dreams?
There he was, young Shelley, all of nineteen,
Out to overthrow the world's tyranny,
Burning to build harmonious Eden.
I see him now just as I must have been –
With fiery eyes and unfettered hope,
And a schedule of miracles for the morning;
Caught in the whirlwind of causes: pamphlets
And politics, parliament and protests.

Sweet are the dreams of youth, my friend, and well
I know the vision calling you to strive
For good. Coleridge and I once had our dreams:
First, the desire to save an insane world,
Physicians to a lunatic nation.
Then bruised and disillusioned, hope displaced
To a different dream, we sought not to change,
But create: to flee a failing country
Like latter-day Adams seeking new Edens;
To find across the ocean a new way
In another world, a still-sylvan land,
To begin again far from the grim truth
We knew. And here I am, in England, still;
Feeding, through endless ink and empty paper,
And the so-far ceaseless spring of running words,
More mouths than an honest gypsy could foretell.
What has happened to my sweet, pretty plan?
The rage of urgency for righteousness?
Shelley calls me hypocrite, apostate,
The enemy of all that I once was;

As if he alone were holy, speaking
With all the arrogance of atheists.
Apostate? No. I do not shout as once
I did. But I am the man I was of old.
My hopes and dreams remain, unabandoned.
And if England's eyes look askance at me,
Perhaps it is that times have changed, not I.
And if my ideas have grown with age,
My heart is where it was, no matter if
Opinions come and go. I have no care
Anymore for the dominion of opinion –
The whole abhorrent business of the press,
The public, and the hunger for power.
I do care for hopes, though hopes are humbled
With the passing of time. I see from where
I stand today beyond fanaticism.
Though the eyes of youth be bright, they are not
Always keen. And thus we see the folly
Of opinions. How often men express
The very best ideals, only to find
When power comes how very foul they are.
In this the French have proved the perfect text.
For passion unbounded may not be pure,
And righteousness seduces well to sin.

If Shelley would listen, my words would be:
Go forth, young fire, but beware your heat.
The light of love can be the flame of hate
If you be not purged of evil. Eden
Is not built by angry men. Perhaps
It is not built at all, except by God.
Stinging words make enemies and not
The peace you seek. Indeed, the peace you seek
Is not found in politics and protests.
Yes, laws may change but never enough,
For you are a secular prophet who seeks
An atheist's Eden. A strange creation.
If God has humor, He must be laughing.

And what world is it that I am building?
A little domestic sanctuary
Where the cannons of battle cannot be heard
And Love becomes embodied in a child.
After all, a child is the only
Evidence of Eden. As Shelley seeks
To establish governments of love
And redeem meandering humanity
From despots, wars, poverty, laws, and lies,
I live within my little world, and if
I call this Eden, Shelley may argue,
But God will understand.

Haydon's Rage

*Benjamin Robert Haydon (1786–1846) was a historical
painter who was friends with Keats, Wordsworth, Hazlitt, and
other notable people of his age. Near the end of his life, while
he rented a hall to exhibit his paintings, P.T. Barnum created
a sensation in London with General Tom Thumb.*

If I were a prophet, I'd speak of doom.
Is it always thus, or has history
Gone wrong? Is every genius in his lifetime
Lost? I have lived with starlight shining
In my soul like a beacon on the horizon,
Summoning me to a sacred calling.
But art in England is profane or dead.
Raphael? Forgotten. Michelangelo?
Not modern. Dear God! Let us reject
The truly great for making us look small.
We shall lower our sights, change our standards,
And claim for our limited selves success
In lesser endeavors. Not I. I have
Measured myself against magnificence,
And if I have failed, still have I striven,
Painting like an angel filled with fury.

The lords and ladies want their portraits done,
And have no use for history that stirs
The blood and wounds the waking soul:
Solomon, the wise, sitting in judgment;
Lazarus rising from darkness to light;
Jesus, triumphant, in Jerusalem;
And Napoleon, defeated, musing
On his fate. Only – "Paint our portraits, please.
We'd rather gaze all day upon ourselves."
And miniatures they want – the littlest things
That ever hung, while I stretched my canvas
For works that would cover a castle wall,
As large as sails on ships that cross the seas.
Or they want landscapes – pretty little things,

Something tame to decorate a corner.
Their eyes are open, but their vision blank,
Blind to the grandeur of man's agony,
The spirit grappling against fate, and beauty
That transcends the pretty and the tame.

But this! This is a bullet to my brain.
Tom Thumb! A little finger of a man!
Twelve thousand this week to see a midget!
While my paintings hang in an empty hall,
Ignored by a world that has turned its back
On the eternal, the frantic masses flock
Like fevered sheep to feed upon a dwarf –
Shouting, panting, pushing – desperate
To see this Thumb! Why? Because he is small.
Because the small makes men feel falsely large.
Because he is new and history is old.
Because the trivial is quick, while greatness
Asks for patience and long labor. Exaltation
Is not easy; fulfillment is elusive;
And little men know nothing of the largeness
Of the soul. Let us all be little men.
Let no one dare, let none aspire.
Let us cage ourselves in a little world.
We shall be entertained, not awe-struck.
Amused, not moved. We shall celebrate
The safety of the harbor, not the surging
Of the sea. Let Tom Thumb be our god.

Year after year of labor, with little
Triumphs and long disappointments – struggling
Against poverty, against obscurity,
Against failing eyesight too long punished
By painting endless hours by dim candles.
Four times condemned to prison for my debts,
Driven to degrade my art to feed
My family. Five times to the graveyard
To bury a child. For the others,
I thank God that they have been spared the spark
Of art, for they shall live far better lives
Than artists amid dust and suffering.
If I had been recognized and acclaimed
What different path were mine, what different end?

What heights might I have reached without the press
Of poverty? Without the rush to finish
And find a buyer, to gain some cash,
To hound the market to obtain the coin
To carry on and again seek greatness?
Decade upon decade I have struggled.
But, God forgive me, my struggles are done.
Now, which shall it be – the razor, or gun?

Beethoven Besieged

In May, 1809, Vienna was besieged and then occupied by Napoleon's forces. Beethoven's work was interrupted as he was forced to take shelter. Beethoven had admired Napoleon until the latter crowned himself emperor, betraying the hope of the French Revolution.

Damn the soldiers! Damn their cannon! Damn them all!
And damn you, too, Napoleon, who
Carried hope so high. How far the mighty fall
When the taste of power, like insidious brew,
Lays siege upon the soul, and a man's best nature
Surrenders to the tyranny of greed.
May your heart burst, if ever you remember
What once you were, before the victory of pride
Vanquished all the truths that should have ruled.

How strong you are, oh little man, who takes
His strength from armies in his pay. And yet,
Damn it! The bastard has some magic that makes
The world turn upon his calling. I hate
To grant him genius, but Europe quakes
With his footsteps. Balanced in the scale,
I am nothing – note-scribbler, sound-maker,
Player of keys; besieged by a lunatic's hell
Of lust for conquest and barbarous rule.

But in the balance of nobility I am gold
To his baseness, for he is one who celebrates
Himself as the peak and pilot of the world,
And rides the earth as his carriage unto greatness.
He is a little man commanding lesser men
To evil; a genius of violence who brings
Destruction, chaos, and corpses in his reign
Of madness; sailing on his vulture's wings
He sees only what is to be devoured – insatiable king.

He's a decorated ghost; an emptiness
Craving recognition; a hungry fire
Ever feeding on its own inadequacies;
A man so prodigal in his desire
He consumes the blood of nations, and still
Needs more, surrounding himself with wealth
And worship. Nothing will ever fulfill
Such a man. While I am, within myself,
All I need, if only I could escape this hell.

What a pity – if I knew the ways of war
Like the making of music – ah, but no;
His world is one of blood and plots, murder,
Politics, territory, domination. And though
He must be countered, I want no part
Of such a world, and I pay for it with fear.
And that is why I sit in this damp and dark,
Huddled in a basement, praying for peace,
Wakened by the bombing from my dreams.

Where in this desolation is there peace
To create and bring glory out of chaos?
What place for me, when the world wants bullets
More than beauty? Am I not, too, a genius?
Sovereign of my own domain? Who with divine
Art brings invisible kingdoms to earth?
Then why am I employed by little men
Of lesser worth who pass their titles on like crowns
For any head to wear that bears the luck of birth?

Nobility by birth – bah! Princes come and go,
But there is only one Beethoven, and I
Have built my own nobility. I will not bow
To any man – let Napoleon call me
For an audience and see. I wonder –
Will he call? Does he know my name? Does his thought
Ever turn to me? Perhaps, but no matter;
Better not to be interrupted – I must write,
And he's nothing but a nuisance to my art.

And yet, he, too, from an opening obscure
Has lived a long crescendo – a common man
In France, rising to ultimate power.
And now the world awaits the unforeseen
Finale. His defeat will be the nations' gain,
For though his name has taken history
And will make it speak of him, his guns
Are set against the will of God and men, and he
Stirs their hearts to hatred, who seek but to be free.

The idol stands revealed for what he is,
And now I see no human can sustain
Worship's burden. And I cannot forgive
His smug corruption of the hope of men.
What fate awaits him and what fame,
I cannot say. Perhaps the world will learn
There are other roads to glory. Time
Will show what force endures the storm,
When once this tide retreats, and we to life return.

Professor Libri's Lament

*Libri was a professor at the University of
Padua, Italy, in the year 1610.*

The heavens have exploded to chaos!
Six months ago the earth stood firm – the spheres
Of sun, moon, planets, and all patterned stars
Were fixed, ordered, closed, and known; all precise
In concept, secure in the firmament
As spoken by the witness of Scripture,
And therefore holy and assured. But now,
New planets, countless stars, revolutions,
Rotations – dear God, they say the earth moves!
Against Scripture and all evidence of sense –
The earth move? Moving round the sun? The sun
Now the center and not God's favored earth?
The earth cast out as peripheral rock,
A spinning plot shorn of all foundation.

The heavens were all immutable and pure,
Free from earth's taint of change and decay.
But now the very sun is blemished – spots
Like pestilence confound our source of light.
The moon is craggy, mountainous – not pure
At all, but looking even like the earth.
If heavenly lights be flawed, what of us?
If we be not in the center, then where?
New planets, new stars – stars beyond all thought –
The seven bright sisters of the Pleiades
Are now forty-three in number, or such
Was the last I heard; perhaps more will come.

Gossip now is of traveling to the moon,
And other planets, and if Eden be
Elsewhere as it was on earth, and if God
Made distant, different Adams there to dwell.
Can it be? Can creation thus be common?
Are we no longer alone? Oh, where then

Is God? I am sick, old, and soon to die –
I thought it was a short and simple path
For the soul's ascent from earth to heaven,
But all is now confusion and despair –
To what wandering sphere commend my spirit?
Now one needs geometry and numbers,
A celestial map drawn by the Imperial
Mathematicus himself to calculate
A course through jumbled heaven unto God.
Where is this weary spirit bound?

I had a chance to see, once, through a scope,
But deemed Galileo madman or charlatan,
Sure his fantasies would fade to nothing.
I was wrong. I refused the opportunity
To see a new and different sky, afraid
Only that I would. Some who are devout
Claim it as the latest of revelation,
A new unveiling of divinity,
The truth of the universe now made known
By those odd prophets, the men of learning;
The triumph of the light of truth over
Error and backward darkness of the past.
But why the contradiction with Scripture?
What place is there for faith when all is changed?
What heaven and hell for a spinning ball
Hurtling like other planets – who knows how
Many – around a flawed and changing sun?
Truth – truth I do not need so much as sense;
I'm old – I cannot feed my soul on facts.
Is there nourishment in calculations,
Sightings, theories – can some new telescope
Find meaning in orbits, God in the stars?
New revelation? No, I cannot see it;
All I see is the sudden shattering
Of grandeur. Will this new way make men more wise
Or virtuous? Galileo is full
Of arrogance, conceit, self-exaltation –
If this be an omen, it bodes not well.

If new things can come, can these be the last,
Or will further changes make these new truths
But temporary and soon to be displaced?

And will they then really have been truths at all?
What age of chaos are we coming to
When truth is not eternal and divine,
But subject to a man with glass and metal
In his hand, and self-magnitude in mind?
This is no priest or prophet I can follow.

Four new planets – all around Jupiter –
As strange as thinking the very earth moves.
Please write with words of comfort if you can.
Your faithful and perplexed friend, Libri.

Stone-Killer Robinson

As told by the Reverend Dr. William Stukeley, an
antiquarian who studied the stone circles of Stonehenge
and Avebury, and watched the destruction of the latter
by Robinson and his followers in the mid-1700s.

A civil man am I and slow to wrath;
Tempered by intellect, sustained by faith;
An unmoved atom in a mob's angry mass;
Each passion balanced in its proper place.
Antiquities in stone are all my love,
And all the learning that I hope to leave.
Their longevity will outlast my blood,
But on their age my fleshless name shall feed.
Unless this villain and his devils spread
Their frenzy, and great works the ancients made
Are lost, corrupted into chaos, by men
Who lose themselves in fevers of the brain.

This is sad; sad to me as is a death:
To witness the destruction of the one, true faith.
Ah, ye Druids! Who raised with long devotion
Stones that stud the earth across Salisbury Plain!
Whose unremembered mind conceived the massive plan
Of Avebury, whose grand design hides within
Its lines and rings a forgotten covenant?
My eyes wander over this monument,
Enchanting as tunes in a foreign tongue
Whose words are strangers and stir me to sing,
But leave me no wiser when they are done,
Though surer there's something stirring within.

Ah, what words would you speak, elusive runes?
What will has written thus upon our plains?
Illiterate age! Without the sense or shrewder
Skill to read this language lost in these later
Days. And more than large stones have been aligned:
The ancients shaped hills with an artist's hand,
Made valleys and plains more pleasing to their sight.
They shared creation of their land, like that
Of the Orient, where contrary forces blend
And every stream and meadow is designed:
The dragon paths, the landscape's nerves, that set
The spirit free to soar through dark and light.

Exalted prayer made manifest in earth!
Who are these who come to break your solemn oath
With God? Men of decadence! Who will defend
Your temple, when there is only I – disowned
By the village, a voice crying aloud
In a soul-less void, as vast and wild
As any that ever made Isaiah shout
With righteous anger. "Stone-killer!
Ignorant bastard! Pride-possessed disease!
Who speaks holy words, blind to holy ways.
'Pagan stones!' you cry; pagan to a fiend
Who leads dull, crusading fools ordained
In devastation. Robinson! Your name
Is black, and thus shall your memory become.
A barbarous, petty chieftain, you reign
Mightily, and mightily have you won
A battle with a rock that had no quarrel
With you. The Pleiades fade in a swirl
Of smoke, rising to darken the sky, bright-starred.
Your pious savages await the word
To topple the monolith into flames –
Their little, local, homemade hell. Sing hymns
Of forgiveness, for if words could conjure, I'd pray
For a warrior Druid to pounce with vengeance
On your flesh, batter your bones with club and stone,
Return the violence you have waged, and burn
Your soul with agony. If you will destroy,
Expect the visitation of your sins upon you.
Conquer now, but reap the harvest of your hate,
And suffer in the prison of your sins.
Claim victory by violence, seek order

Through force; command conformity, but never harmony.
Your triumph will ring hollow in Time's ears,
And down the corridors of history, I pray,
This little war of wisdom and desire
Will not be forgotten."

The great stone falls to its fiery grave,
And as it massively slants in its solemn dive,
Like a conquered Titan cast into flame,
A host of sparks rush up like stars to climb
Their way to heaven, but perish in the night.
The toppled stone takes in the fire's heat,
Then icy water pierces like a spike
The burning rock, and with a demon's shriek
A heavy hammer smites the tortured stone,
Breaking my heart, and shattering the one
Grand monolith to fragments in a hole.
'More, more!' they yell, for hate's insatiable.

They only know fire and ice as foes,
They only know stones as their enemies;
Their passion burns, but warms not a soul,
Consumed in a flame that never will heal.
These contours of land were divinely drawn,
This world was a temple, rugged and fine.
There was reverence, then, as I read the lore,
And knowledge, too, at one with desire.
The Druids lived in a land that we now live on,
Intertwined in a world from earth to sun.
The wisdom of their worship genders awe,
And a sense of wonder lived to the full.

Once, in moonlit vision I beheld the design:
The serpent through the circle, the dragon
And egg; this plan of rings and lines defied
All eyes, being for twenty centuries hid.
Confirmed in my faith, my soul rose to sing;
I forgot Stone-killer and all his gang.
I was learning the language that once had been
The union of cultures and natures of man.
Faced with a majesty ancient and new,
I was a peasant, still humble and low.
I had read my first word by the light of the moon,
Inscribed in this page of the earth with stone.

The Descendants of Cain

¶ Based on a dream of Samuel Taylor Coleridge's

Old Adam, when his days were growing few;
When Eden, like a morning dream, was little more
Than vague emotion, and a sense that long before
He held a truth he now no longer knew;

When thus he wandered homeless through the land,
He came into a town, filled with a noisy crowd,
Busy at the market, with language harsh and loud,
Involved in things he did not understand.

"This is the town of the people of Cain,
Who died long ago. We still honor him with praise
And blessings, and follow the wisdom of his ways,
Who taught us that the earth is for our gain.

"Who are you, old man? What is it you say?
A foreigner, no doubt; I never heard a tongue
Like yours. Listen, old man, if you want to feel young,
I have good women here, if you can pay."

"I am Adam, made by the Lord,
Brought forth in glory from spirit and earth;
I walked with the Lord in the land of my birth,
Till banished by a flaming sword.

"I was a man when the world had but one;
Alone, till the miraculous making of Eve –
God's greatest work, I still believe;
She brought forth children – Cain was our son."

"I can't understand – what's the old fool say?"
"He's either crazy or playing some game
To cheat us by using our founder's name."
"Liar or madman, let's make the fool pay."

The child of God from Eden's fair light,
Who witnessed the world when the world was new,
Remembered beginnings and tried to be true,
Was caught by the crowd and killed in the night.

Fergus and the Thorn-Tree

Fergus is a character in Scottish folklore. This
story is from the island of Iona.

Dark green the wet grass and dark gray the stone,
Mist on the cold moor and branches like bone,
And dark the young heart of Fergus is grown.

Stories are told of the old withered thorn,
Witch-like it whispers to burden or mourn;
Do not go near if you be not forlorn.

Never approach with a heart bright as gold –
All joy will wither and warmth turn to cold;
Youth, too, will fade and the world all be old.

Dark-hearted lovers may pass without care,
Long having walked through the hell of despair;
Of whispered sorrows they need not beware.

Now Fergus, the moon, the mist, and the tree,
Met on the moor and kept good company,
Moonlight and silence beside the cold sea.

The thorn had a small stalk, hollow and dry,
With holes like a pipe that caught Fergus' eye,
For he could play tunes to make cold hearts cry.

He plucked it and played till the mist cleared away,
And night was replaced by the brightness of day,
And autumn itself was changed into May.

The desolate winter that kept the tree stark,
Broke, and white blossoms appeared on the bark,
Bright with green leaves over-spreading the dark.

Never the thorn had put forth such fine fruit,
As now sweetly bloomed from deep-reaching root,
Let loose by Fergus who played the black flute.

Sorrowful song is a joy and a sigh,
Moonlight and mist and a tear in the eye,
From darkness to light with a heart-breaking cry.

Sad the song played, but sadder it passed;
Brief as a candle, the breath cannot last;
Black the tree turned in the cold wind's blast.

Fergus returned to his home by the sea,
Gray sky and water and gray heart had he,
But folk still tell of his time with the tree.

The Destruction of Wilhelm Reich

Reich began his career as a psychoanalyst under Freud. Later, he
conducted research on what he called orgone energy. In 1956, the
Food and Drug Administration of the United States began a smear
campaign against him, which resulted in the burning of some of his
writings and the destruction of his equipment. He was subsequently
sent to prison, where he died in 1957. He is speaking here to the
man who supervised the chopping up of his equipment with axes.

Going so soon? No, you are not finished.
I have books. I have papers. They will burn.
They will make a nice fire, no? I will
Bring them to you. I really must insist.
I want to help you in the work you do.
Such important work, to ruin a man.
Men like me come once in a thousand years.
It is an honor to bring great men down.
A shame that you missed Giordano Bruno.
You would have been a help with his burning.

What? Bruno? You never heard of Bruno?
I didn't think so. Jesus, you know, yes?
You have heard? Jewish man? Long ago? Killed?
This much you know? Such a smart fellow.
So, did you enjoy the crucifixion?
How was it to hang a man on a cross?
Quite exciting, I imagine. Perhaps
The height of your low life, to crush a man
Who could have changed the world. For change, of course,
Is such a messy matter. Better to keep
Things as they are and commit a little
Murder.
            What? Of course you were alive then.
You are always alive. You or your kind.
Frightened men. Frightened of the life within.
Your fear rules you and you rule the world.
And because you are afraid of what I am,

You murder me just as you have murdered
Jesus.
        Yes, you're right. You have not killed me.
But you will. You, or another like you.
You cannot let me live. It is not safe.
I speak of things you do not want to hear.
Better to silence me, or I might speak
Of love. Even worse, sex. Or of the joy
That is our birthright. But no, too much light
Is dangerous. You should stay in your cave.
You will keep me in your cave till I die.
Only, you cannot keep me. I'm too strong.
You call this persecution? Hah. I've been
Run out of five countries. You want lessons
In oppression? Talk to Nazis. They know.
This is nothing. You can break my machines,
But you cannot break me. You can kill me,
And you will have to, because I won't stop.
I have a vision. Not just a vision.
I am a scientist. I have data.
I have found the world's primal energy.
I have not mastered it, but I've found it.
I can work with it. Perhaps you need help?
You seem a sad man, a shameful man.
Where is your strength? Where is your passion?
Most importantly, where is your joy?
You hang your head. Even at the threshold,
In the presence of one who could bring change,
You shy away. Yes. Perhaps you are right.
Change is dangerous. Yes. Stay in your cave.
For me, I shall seek the sunlight – always,
Until you strike me dead. You and all the others.
I offer you the key to the prison,
But freedom is so very hard to bear.
So your frightened soul builds walls within
To block its own desires. And you block me,
Because prisoners hate those who are free.
Pardon? Yes, you are sorry. So am I.
We are all sorry. It is not your fault.
No. Of course not. What is one to do?
You are human, and humans are so weak.
But it is the weak who are dangerous.
The weak who kill. The weak who crucify.

The weak seek power. The strong seek life.
Strength does not crush. It lifts, it liberates.
You're sorry. Perhaps one day you will see.
My books are burned because I speak the truth.
If I were wrong, I'd be ignored. At least
I am in good company, for you burned
Bruno, too. But then, you don't remember.
It is for the best. Repression works well.
Your defenses will always protect you.
You're a lucky man. With a little work,
You could be invulnerable as the dead.
But then, you are dead already. Get out.

Elizabeth

For Elizabeth Randall-Mills: poet and friend, 1906–1993.

No, Peter, I am not at all "okay."
I hurt my writing arm – I had a fall.
The crazy doctor gave me this old cane,
As if to say I'd somehow walk again,
As if hope could help postpone what has come.
"It's rather fun to be seventy-five" –
Do you remember when I told you that?
Years ago, it was. I can't say it now.
But I mustn't be morose. I shall smile,
And say how kind of you it is to come
And mind an old woman low in spirits.
It means so much these days, living alone.
My husband's long dead, and never any
Children – so who will follow where I walk
And greet my special trees by name?
I do imagine them as friends, you know.
For forty years we've watched each other live.
To me they are the richness of this world;
I like to think they brighten with my coming,
And come I have, each day, for forty years.
It's not so lonely with trees for friends.
The flowers come and go too fast to know;
And so many – daffodils and lilies –
We barely get acquainted in a season.

Today I name you keeper of the trees,
To follow when I'm gone and speak with them,
For I shan't walk again. It hurts me so.
My favorite maple I can see from here;
It flames as if with passion in the fall.
But the others, so many others –
The old, knotted willow, with its branches
Like a young girl's hair; the three thin birches;
The row of hemlocks by the bridge – you know,
They look like dark, hooded figures – like saints

In line to sing a chorus up to God.
I think we must believe in God, don't you?
Without God and trees I'd have no poems –
What else is worth the writing?
Yes, love, of course, and sorrow. A few things.
A worthy task for poets, don't you think?
To honor Glory with enduring words,
And to speak the human things of the soul.
I wish you could keep my friends company
For more than this little visit. I guess
That when I'm gone you will not come again
To so remote a place. I understand.
I'm still bothered by my body's weakness,
Though today it doesn't seem quite so bad.
Maybe I will walk again. After all,
Autumn is near, the maple is turning red.
I want to stand beneath it as before,
And gaze up through the colors at the sky.
And I so love autumn; yes, spring and fall,
Youth and maturity – the times of passion;
First of the flesh and earthly things; and now,
A different longing and a different love.
Yes, Peter, I will rise again, I know.
Whether to walk the path by the river,
Or cross to another realm, I will rise.
Broken bones won't keep me down forever.

Please come here once, at least, when I am gone,
And walk again the path we always go.
I wish I could hear your poetry then;
But when I'm alone I'll smile and think
There's beauty still to come. Ah, poetry,
A lovely task, and always more to do.
Come – give me your arm – the trees are waiting.

Jamie Macdonald's Love

❡ A story from western Scotland that occurred in the 1800s

Jamie would watch the gulls and the gray sea
Through my window, or maybe he saw nothing
But all the old ghosts who haunted his days,
As he told of his first love and long sorrow –
How Jean Cameron gave him his only kiss,
And they pledged their hearts to always be true.
Ah, but he went away into the war,
And soon word came that he had died.

                                            Of course,
With "J. Macdonalds" being like thistles
In spring – all over everywhere – mistakes
Were bound to happen. And Jeanie, poor girl,
Cried and cried until she could cry no more,
Believing that Jamie was dead and gone.
And in her grief she married, and not well.
And back comes Jamie from afar, and Jean's
Heart broke again, and worse than before. And if
Your days seem sometimes dark, there was Jamie,
Back from whatever hell there is in war,
Come for his happiness so long waiting,
To find her with another.

                                "Let her go,"
They told him – all his friends – and took him out
To drink, and talked of all the world's women,
How many there were and his for choosing.
But only, there was no letting her go.
He held no blame, and told her he would be true.
And many a friend winked a knowing wink,
And laughed and waited. And they're still waiting,
If they haven't died by now, for Jamie
Never found another, finding comfort
Knowing he was the one man in her heart,
Though another was in her home. And bad
He was, this other one. To jail he went,
And there he stayed. And Jean with three young ones.
But James Macdonald had given his word,

And he gave to Jean whatever he could
To feed the children that were not his own,
Though he had but little himself.

                         His friends
All shook their heads and called him doubly daft,
And pitied him for living in a dream.
And all the while I think he pitied them,
For missing what to him was very plain.
He makes you wonder, Jamie does, what longings
Lie in a man's heart? I could have asked him,
But if I know Jamie, he would have just
Shrugged his big shoulders, looked out at the sea,
And mumbled something simple about love.

The MacPhersons and the Seal

On the western coast of Scotland there are many tales of "seal-people" or silkies. In some tales, humans become friends with the seal-people. In others, humans become seal-people and can change back and forth from seals to humans.

"Angus, I did not want to trouble you,
 But it is troubled I am, and you should
 Know how the town-folk talk of our Mary –
 How she keeps to herself and goes somewhere
 Away, and at the dances is not seen,
 And how she pays no mind to any boy.
 You can sing her praises and sing them long,
 But Mary is not like all other folk."

"And glad you should be that she is not so.
 Would you rather she took up with some boy –
 Some young trouble, and came home with child?
 She likes to go to the island alone –
 Don't we all need rest and a place apart?
 After the fishing's done and she's tired
 Of nets and chores and work and still more work,
 If play she wants, or rest, or peace, I say
 Let the girl be."

             "Och, but Angus, my dear,
 You are not in town to hear the tongues talk.
 And it is getting worse. They sometimes think
 That maybe she's not right – that something's wrong
 More than simply liking to be alone.
 And I wonder, too, don't you know. I mean,
 That island – what is it day after day
 She does, and why is it when she returns
 She seems to almost glow with secret joy?"

"Why not ask why more of us cannot find
  Such joy? Or why the town-folk cannot find
  More proper talk than a young girl's joy, though
  Different it be?"

                    "Angus, please, for me,
  Find out what it is she does – follow her –
  And let me know that it is nothing strange.
  Let the people talk, but let me have peace."

"Dear woman, you let the people poison
  Your love, till you have no faith in Mary.
  Och, woman, I will go, so I'll have peace
  From your worries, and you'll not trouble me
  As the talking town-folk have troubled you."

                    ∾

"Angus, you're back – and did you find it out –
  What it is our Mary does?"

                    "I found out.
  I followed her footprints and heard her laugh,
  And her voice was like the great wave that breaks
  Upon the rock, leaping high in sunlight,
  And falling softly down. Ay, and if I
  Could laugh like sunlight and the swelling sea,
  I'd have no need of heaven. So on I went,
  Wondering what could bring from a lass such sound.
  Let the tongues gossip as they always will,
  But put your worries away. There she was,
  Our sweet Mary, playing with a young seal.
  That only, and nothing other. Perhaps
  She found it as a pup and cared for it,
  As she often does with other creatures.
  I don't know. But there she was and happy,
  And I breathed better seeing it myself."

"Angus, I'm thinking that that was not a seal,
But a silkie. You know Grandmother's tales,
How the seal-people lure young folk away.
They take to the waves and are not seen again.
Mary's bewitched, she is under a spell.
If you love your daughter, kill the silkie,
Or we'll lose her to the sea's enchantments."

"If that's bewitching, may it spread to us all.
What if there's nothing amiss in Mary?
What if the town-folk are under a spell
Of their own making? If I love Mary?
Ay, I love her, and I'll not take away
Her joy. Kill the seal? It would break her heart."

"Ay, and it will break yours and mine to see
Her go, and not come back. Can you not see?
The life she's been living – it isn't right.
Och, she's sweet and kind and always a help –
But it isn't natural – going off –
With no human friends, alone with a seal.
Listen well, Angus MacPherson, my man.
I will not cook for you nor clean; there'll be
No speech between us nor no love; I will
Leave this house and leave you as well, unless
You kill the silkie. Just a seal, you say?
Very well. There are seals by the thousands.
If her heart breaks, find another young seal.
But if I'm right, and the enchantment passes,
Then we'll not lose our daughter to the sea,
And she will live as all the others,
And the tongues will stop and my heart have rest."

≈

"Woman! I did the deed and may I die!
To the island I went and found the seal.
I raised my gun and shot. I saw the blood.
The seal cried and hobbled to the water,
Maybe to die. And something inside me
Went all hollow, and trembled, like I'd done
A crime; like I had murdered something dear.
Weak I am, and shaking. I feel some dread,

Like the devil's hand were on my shoulder,
Making me cold. It is a fearful thing.
Let me lie down. What have I done? A drink –
Bring me a drink. Ah, guilt is upon me
Like a shadow. Are you happy, woman?"

∾

"Angus, when Mary left for the island,
I told her nothing of what you had done.
Maybe she'll think the seal went on its way
With other seals. Maybe she will not mind
So very much. I only wish she'd come.
She went out early. Many hours now
It is that she's been gone. She's never stayed
So long before. But then, she must be sad.
I hate to think she's crying all alone.
Angus, why don't you go and bring her home?
It's comforting she'll be needing."

∾

                    "Woman!
I'll curse the day forever I listened
To your talk, and killed my own daughter's joy.
No, I did not bring Mary home. There is
No Mary to bring home, I'm a-thinking.
Ay, her boat was there and her footprints, too.
She found the blood and her steps followed it
Into the sea. Now maybe all your talk
And grandmother's tales have me all but daft,
But out in the water I saw two seals,
And their dark eyes looked into mine with something
Clear and pure that pierced me, and when they dived
My heart sank with them into the cold sea,
And I knew Mary was not coming home."

Oran from Iona's Shore

Iona is a tiny island off the west coast of Scotland, where
St. Columba founded a monastery in 563 CE. Oran
was a monk there many centuries ago.

If this tale you would hear, keep it with care:
One man is dead who did not beware.

>"Oran from Iona's shore
> Went north alone to find the pole.
> Oran now goes forth no more;
> Say a prayer for Oran's soul."

Oran was young and bright and quick to dare;
He slipped out one night from the evening prayer;
From light of the chapel to unlit moor,
Closing behind him the thick wooden door.
He followed the smooth path, grassless and dead,
Lost in adventure inside his young head.
He strayed from the path and stood on the shore,
And gazed at the night where as never before,
The stars, the sea, and the ships all were fair,
With moonlight on water, windy and clear.
Restless for more than old words for his soul,
He boarded a ship and sailed for the pole.

>"Thrice seven days through snow and ice
> He sliced through frozen seas;
> And still he sailed, thrice thirty days,
> Though all his sails did freeze.

>"Fearless he went, for thrice three years –
> The tears on his cheeks all froze;
> Whipped by the wind, his once bright eyes
> Surrendered their sight, and closed."

Oran sailed through strange seas, still unafraid,
Welcomed by strangers who came to his aid.
He was served by fish a drink of the deep,
Soothing as waves and the rhythm of sleep.
And shimmering birds like flames in their flight,
Guided like beacons amid the dark night.
Then, gentle as breath, brave angels alone,
Sang and sustained him in places unknown.
Or almost unknown, for Oran, of course,
Knew tales of the folk who dwell at the source
Of all cold, where the chill wind is born,
Where now he awoke feeling empty and worn.

His eyes were pierced by a bright paradise,
An endless shining of blue sky and ice.
He stood amid cities that shimmered like dreams
Where icebergs glisten and moonlight gleams;
Where seasons are brief, where dawn is an age,
Where wisdom is wild and innocence sage.
The craft of the fairies was cunning and rare,
Inspired to weave designs from despair.
Their world was beauty untainted by sin,
As if visions endured and they lived therein.
A city was built of a wind that sings,
And one of bright fire whose flame never stings;
And fountains of water like crescents of light,
Leaping and sparkling like diamonds in flight.
And last, a city built of earth and stone,
With wonders unguessed, where he now made his home:
Where all roads meet, at the center of space,
Is the valley that keeps the secret of grace:
In joy and reverence pilgrims refresh
Sacred spirit and sacred flesh.

Three hundred years with the timeless folk,
Until the day came when Oran awoke,
And found himself home on Iona's shore,
Back to the place he left long before.
With eyes like a prophet's, wild and bright,
He saw where he was, but saw more than sight;
Vision was lifting the veil of his mind,
Half trapped in glory and half earth-confined.
Astride two realms, he crawled to the door

Of the chapel he left the night before.
The monks surrounded him, and he spoke
With innocent frenzy of mystical folk.

"Ah, my dear friends, you cannot conceive
The beauty I found. Come, let us leave
This rock surrounded by sea,
Come to the north where spirits are free.
The men and women surpass loveliness;
Their speech is music knowing only to bless.
The love in their eyes arose and took wing,
And love, too, I knew in the flowers of spring.
Thirst was a passion, fulfillment delight,
Hungry affections were shared in the night.
God's glorious image, in humans revealed,
Brought deeper devotion and emptiness healed.
Torches are lit with the fire of stars,
And at the full moon, with Venus and Mars,
The folk go to battle and all shadows slay,
Laughing and leaping amid their bright play.
Peace between people and peace within each –
There is the gospel we earnestly preach.
Come, let us go, I can show you new ways
To deliver us all from the chains of our days."
The monks were silent – scared or sad;
The oldest spoke first: "The man is mad."
"And dangerous," said one, and all agreed.
They bound him in rope with hideous speed,
And dug up the earth to make a great hole,
And put Oran in for the good of his soul.
The old monk spoke, rigid and grim:
"You have been to a world of devils and sin.
You were enticed and your soul is in Hell;
Return to the realm where your spirit fell.
For you and the fiends there is torment and death.
Tell them to come and submit to our faith."
Oran was buried alive in the earth,
But none of the folk ever came from the north.

I know the story of that strange night,
For I, too, left prayer and kept Oran in sight.
Across the dark hill and down to the shore,
Pulled by an urging surpassing my fear.
I was a child who watched him set sail;
I found him at dawn, unconscious and pale.
Only I heard the whole story he knew;
I witnessed the evil that bitter men do.
I wrote the words to the song I spoke,
Though still it's forbidden to speak of the folk.
I kept the knowledge that somewhere they dwell,
But how Oran found them, my song cannot tell.

    "Oran from Iona's shore
    Went north alone to find the pole.
    Oran now goes forth no more;
    Say a prayer for Oran's soul."

John Lambton and the Worm

The encounter between Lambton and the worm took place in the River Wear in Durham, England, in the early 1400s.

I Prologue

The old ones know the story of the worm:
The demon's death and prophecy's alarm;
The blessed knight and his accursed line;
The broken vow, and generations nine
Slain by triumph's turning unforeseen
To tragedy. And like a lurking dream
Surviving darkness into dawn's bright air,
The tale remains. Out of the River Wear
There comes no more of evil to repel,
But it troubles like a nearness unto Hell.

II The Young Fisherman

John Lambton in his youth was less than holy,
Heir to a castle, and to melancholy,
Mixing solitude with unseemly sport;
Idle games and vain pursuits, the sort
The solemn neighbors whisper of and nod,
Knowing how well they keep the ways of God.
The townfolk saw John's ways and predicted ill
Would come, as the best prophets always will.
And if these people knew the ways of God,
Going always in fear of His promised rod,
John had knowledge the others did not wish,
For John was knowing in the ways of fish.
John knew the Commandments and agreed they were good,
But knew no law against searching the wood
For unfound streams and secret pools,
And sun on the water like liquid jewels,
Where a man can dream of being a king,
Even find, perhaps, an untasted spring,
Or dredge from the depths where sight doesn't go
Fish bred in darkness and lurking below.

Now John was fishing on the Sabbath-day,
The clearest sign of morals in decay,
And judging from the looks of those at chapel,
You'd think he'd eaten Eden's second apple.
John hooked a good one, his rod bent double;
He yelled first with delight, then with trouble;
For this was no salmon leaping in air,
But a brute pulling deep, seeking its lair.
Determined to know the manner of beast,
As prophets' dreams are pursued by a priest,
Relentless until the mystery is known,
So John persisted until he had won.
The beast writhed on shore, its great tail flapping,
Sounding on sand like hideous clapping.
Ugly it was, and slippery of form,
As if something molten and still a bit warm
Had not quite hardened and taken its shape,
But came out deformed and made its escape.
Impressed and repelled and a little scared,
John looked at the creature and then declared,
"Why truly I think I've caught the devil!"
This was a mystery none could unravel.
With all Adam's naming, nothing came near
To fitting this beast from a deeper sphere.
The thing was black and slimy and it stank;
It was dropped in a well – it splashed and sank.
Though John forgot about the loathsome beast,
His fishing on the Sabbath ceased.

III   The Warrior

John met the years of manhood unafraid –
Bathed in holy water and joined a crusade
With others seeking fortune or renown,
Or simply to escape the quiet town.
Why John went had something to do with truth
And righteousness, and much to do with youth.
To sustain his heart amid the battle,
He swore an oath to stay in the saddle,
And die or succeed – or be damned. Such vow
Was the strongest the church would allow.
His valor grew, but not his certitude,
As doubt and duty fought a bitter feud.
For the brutal killing brought no reward

But sickness of slaying to please a lord.
Confronted with danger, corruption and death,
A doubter surrounded by violent faith.
Blood was in his nightmares, great pools of blood,
With swords and severed limbs on shoals of mud.
Glory wore a hideous, deformed face,
Savage where his soul was seeking grace.
Hurt deep in his heart, he promised to play
At killing no more, and never more slay.
Sir John, bereft of youth, returned to home,
To be stunned by a strange and threatening doom
That greeted his arrival in the town.

IV Returning Home

In Durham, the calm River Wear winds down
At last to meet the sea; but where it starts,
Not even John had traced to foreign parts,
To find the source and his thirst fulfill,
And follow it faithfully all down hill,
Till the waves come in and the seagulls crowd,
And look back its length to where lost in cloud
The mountain water continues to spring.
And there in the river was the very thing
Young John dropped into a well and forgot.
Grown huge and grown bold, two farmers it caught
And dragged them under and out to sea,
And though God may know where their souls might be,
Their bodies are gone. John's father, in fear,
Kept the great hall shut lest the beast come near;
For though born in water, it ventured on land,
And nothing against the dragon could stand.
The town-folk in horror a vigil kept,
For never the sinister serpent slept.
John's father said: "Have you not heard?
The blacksmith attacked it with lance and sword;
He fought it and dodged it and gouged the skin,
Striking and fighting and struggling to win;
Though skilled with a blade and stout of heart,
He could not prevail, for whatever part
Was cut the beast could mend. Or so the tale
That rumor tells. The man was doomed to fail
For taking on a foe beyond his strength.

He fell on the beach, and the beast's black length
Settled like darkness over fragile light.
It moved like a storm, and then there was night."

Sir John was troubled, and yet he was brave,
So though he felt fear, he wasn't its slave.
He went to study the beast, not to fight;
To see for himself if any man might
Go bravely to battle and come safely home,
And conquer this raging serpent alone.
It lay coiled and curled on an ancient mound,
A marker or beacon or burial ground,
Raised by a people in time dim with age,
Pagans who danced with joy and with rage,
Who opened the door to darkness and sin,
But found more than evil to worship within.
What John beheld with astonished eyes
Staggered his hope with its mammoth size.
The worm, black as night, glistened with sun,
As if mocking the heavenly glow of dawn.
John, being wise in avoiding defeat,
Turned from the beast in his wisest retreat.

v   Seeking Assistance

Durham had a witch, subtle and precise,
Who once built a candle in solid ice,
And then lit the wick through the crystal sheath,
Melting the armor until it could breathe.
A little trick, but striking to behold,
Playing out the battle of hot and cold.
Of course she was ancient, can any witch be young
And be well-versed in magic's mother tongue?
Spells she knew for evil, and healing chants;
How to bless a birth, and how at death to dance.
Laments for broken lovers, and wedding songs,
Elixirs for the trembling to make them strong.
Praise for the sacred, wisdom for grief,
An answer for doubt, and hymns for belief.
For every human circumstance a piece
Of secret knowledge to fulfill or release.

John came to the witch for help in his plight,
He came to her cave on a moonless night,
He came like a shadow, silent and gray,
A whisper of life on its quiet way.
They met, but before he uttered a word,
She hushed him and nodded as if she'd heard
All that was stirring within this young man.
"Come," she said softly, "I have a plan."

She sat by a fire and gazed at its flames,
Chanting in languages all the old names
Creation inspired, and every last thing
That ever moved prophet to curse or to sing.
Her eyes were wide as if watching the sky,
With fire reflected in each wild eye.
The vision she conjured came and passed on;
She blinked her eyes and the moment was gone.

John could no longer deny his voice:
"I must fight the dragon – I have no choice.
I brought the beast from the depths to the day,
The task is my duty, and I must slay
The foul beast or else be destroyed.
My future is fixed, I cannot avoid
The fate I created through wayward youth,
Seeking fulfillment instead of the truth.
Again I must fight till death or success,
Though I go like a beast to sacrifice.
The soul knows the path, and I must obey –
To save the faithful I must again slay.
Perhaps the worm can be conquered by sword,
But what can undo the guilt I incurred
For the farmers and blacksmith killed by the beast –
What haven from horror? What hope for grace?
Speak, please, till all things are clear,
I promise to follow whatever I hear."

VI The Witch's Response

"You speak with assurance of deeds and death,
Lured like a mortal to limited truth.
You brought the beast forth? Did not the beast live?
You created no evil the world did not have.

The battle of man and worm will be long,
Each by the other oppressed and stung.
For good or ill you have chosen your course;
Answers won't help, and they might make things worse.
Come, talk is useless when action is clear;
Adventure's the thing – it's time to prepare."
She gave him a drink of a potion for war
That tasted so bitter he wanted no more.

Down, down she led, down a rock stair
Cut through the mountain and on down to where
A spring formed the root of an ancient river,
Black as a world where night is forever.
She gave him a bright iron suit to wear,
And told him to enter the river with care.
John noisily clanked as he first stepped in,
The rocky dome echoed metallic din,
But John heard no more when the cold touched his skin.
The water was a thousand bitter stings
Of icy snakes with frozen fangs
That bit his hot flesh, till deep in his brain,
Every nerve was screaming its silent pain.
The cold seemed to close on bone and on vein,
Slowing his movements, the flow of his blood,
Till deep in the pool and silent he stood.

The witch slowly nodded her solemn head,
Closed her own eyes, and quietly said:
"Breathe – breathe in the cold, breathe in the pain,
Take it and taste it and feel it again.
You cannot deny, you cannot escape,
Welcome the coldness and seek its embrace.
Think on the blackness, the coldness you feel,
See it and know it and make it more real.
Soundless and still, in stillness endure,
Be nothing but pain, and be the pain pure.
Yes – yes – take it within the grasp of your soul,
Use it as power within your control.
Yes – feel it arise, feel the new fire;
Breathe it in deep, breathe in the desire,
The anguish, the rage,
Building and burning within the cold cage.
Your limbs come alive, your heart cries with heat,

Throbbing your head and eyeballs beat;
Heavy you breathe and faster your pulse,
Dizzying tumult turns in your skull,
Aching to end, to break and release
The fever and agony screaming for peace.
Deep in your soul, from the base of your brain,
Breathe out the torment, breathe out the pain,
Let it sound through the cave,
Let the mountain split,
Let it find the beast's heart
Deep in its pit.
Let your cry be an arrow
From fair thing to foul,
Let it be deadly,
And let it be – NOW!"

With a rush of breath, John threw his head back,
And let out a primitive hideous shriek.
The yell blasted the cave, and echoes returned,
But John kept screaming until his throat burned.
All he knew was the flesh and its shriek;
The world but the sound of a voice in the dark.
The wailing died down, the echoes were gone;
John walked from the water and sat on a stone.
He took off his armor, and weariness crept
Into his being, and then John slept.
The witch, ever-gentle, came and stood near;
She bent down and whispered into his ear:
"Child of water, child of light,
Child of curious, sensitive sight –
Tonight dream of peace,
Dream of angels and ease;
In sleep may you seek
Like a king for a crown,
And find at the peak
That the kingdom is won."

VII Instructions

John woke and told what had passed in his sleep:
"I climbed through a forest thick and steep,
And found a pond that mirrored the sky.
I knelt with joy, content there to die.

108

Bending over, I kissed the warm ground,
I looked in the pool and saw I was crowned
With a golden light around my head –
I looked again, but the light had fled."
The witch nodded and smiled with glittering eyes;
"Good," she said, "but it's time to arise.
What's done is done, but there's always more,
And I can help still, but you must swear
An oath without question – swear to obey –
Follow my words and the beast you will slay.
Put spikes on your armor – front and back.
Stand firm on a stone, and do not attack;
Stand firm on a stone in the midst of the stream;
Stand on a day that is brewing for storm.
Wait for the rain, for the torrent and flood;
Be cold on the skin, but hot in the blood.
The beast's of the water, the river's its home –
Wait for the water to aid in its doom.
One thing more – ask not the cause –
Seek not the knowledge of mystic laws –
If you succeed in slaying the worm,
You also must slay the next living form
That enters your sight." And John said, "I will,
Or forfeit my being for you to kill."
John followed her words and waited for storm;
He arranged if he won to blow a loud horn
For a hound to be freed for him to kill,
To end the ordeal and his promise fulfill.

VIII Triumph and Tragedy

A dark day came, clouds hung low and thick;
John stood still on his stone, his stomach sick.
Alone on a river rising in flood,
White rapids rushing around where he stood.
Then he saw the black beast slide off the shore
And head for the river's turbulent core.
The water covered the stone John was on;
The heat in his heart had faded and gone.
Thunder and lightning and sharp stinging wind;
The current cold on his bright iron skin.
He searched the surface in desperate pursuit –
A splash from behind – the beast grabbed his foot!

He felt the cold slime wind onto his leg,
Tightening with horrible strength; it dragged
His heart down, but still he stood firm,
Resisting the rising of water and worm.
He closed tight his eyes and entered the cold.
He ceased defying and welcomed each fold
Of the grappling beast; he breathed in its stench,
Surrendered a shudder – then his teeth clenched.
In anger he breathed and opened his eyes;
He bellowed a blast of shattering cries.
The gray river ran with ribbons of red –
Pierced by the spikes, self-impaled the beast bled;
It wailed an unearthly, gurgling cry,
Watery rumbling like that of the sky.
The worm in agony writhed and it rolled,
Struggling to loosen its deathly hold.
Ending its torment as it withdrew,
John cut the slippery, slithering horror in two
With one flash of his sword, bright in the dark,
Swinging like lightning and finding its mark.
Half of the beast, awash in its blood,
Was carried away by the force of the flood;
Swept out to sea, it sank and decayed.
And half still hung from a spike on John's leg.
He took it ashore and buried it deep,
Blew loud on his horn, his promise to keep.

John's father was pacing the castle hall;
He froze at the sound of the horn's mighty call.
Then realized it meant the great deed was done,
The dragon was slain, the battle was won.
He ran through the storm to where his son stood
With sword in his hand still dripping with blood.
John's face filled with horror, eyes wide with dread.
The father looked puzzled – was not the beast dead?
Why in his triumph could his son not speak?
Why was he standing there ready to strike?
"No," John muttered, shaking with pain;
"No, no, I cannot; I must be slain."
The father, horror-struck, dropped to the ground –
He'd forgotten to free the promised hound.

ix The Pronouncement

John went to the witch, forlorn and resigned,
And asked for a glass of poisonous wine
To drink and preserve the life of his sire.
The witch gazed into the bright yellow fire,
And said, "You offered your life – I did not ask.
You acted nobly a difficult task,
And faced with the knowledge of breaking your vow,
Chose your course bravely. But what I now
Must speak of your fate is not what I will,
And like things on earth, is both good and ill.
You and your father are both free to live,
But there is a price which many must give
For dealing in magic and slaying the beast,
And breaking the promise of sacrifice.
No lord of the Lambtons who rules the great hall
Shall lie in his bed when death comes to call;
Nobly in battle or tragically drowned,
For nine generations none shall be found
Who surrender to death from age alone.
The fate is decreed by spirit and bone –
They cannot escape it, cannot amend,
Can still seek the path, though where it will end,
And how well they welcome their nothingness,
Awaits to be seen, and I will not guess."

x Descendant Events

The town-folk were glad the creature was dead,
But scarcely grateful to John for his deed.
The name of Lambton took on a queer taint,
And unlike others, he became no saint.
The best that they saw, which wasn't a lot,
Was just the undoing of what he begot.
And it pleased the pious, as they grew old,
That each generation fell as foretold.
The family lived on as the witch said it would,
With glorious deeds of honor and good;
And tragedy, too, but still they survive,
By a witch's promise perhaps kept alive.
The last of the sons on whom the curse fell,
Has now passed away, and who can foretell

What the tenth will be, whether greatest or last,
Now that the magic has finally passed?
The town is still haunted by fear of the beast,
For only Sir John was ever released,
And he by a witch and her odd providence,
And she left long ago and has not been seen since.

LYRICS
& SONNETS

The Messenger

The old man used to dream of being chased,
But he never knew by whom, or what – ghost
Or angel. And sometimes, when all alone
And towards the end, the dreams would leave his brain
And be suddenly behind him in the woods,
Or on a path at night amid the shades
Of darkness. The old man felt a pain
Akin to panic, and hurried to be gone.
He knew the thing that chased him meant no harm –
It was a voice within a ghostly form;
As if a god or spirit from ages gone
Sought to deliver a word to the man.
But the old man never dared to wait,
Whether awake or in dream, to stop and meet
The messenger who gave him so much fear,
To find death or salvation, hope or despair.
He wanted to – he wished that he were brave;
He even thought that if he had the nerve
To stand and bear the voice, that what he heard
Would finish something that was still unmade.
But he outran the footsteps in his soul,
And never faced the ages at his heel;
Perhaps the messenger had little to reveal;
Perhaps he had the words to make him whole.

The Flame of Faith

Yes, he's found faith; no doubt a great relief.
He acts as if the shadows are all gone.
There's a light, that if not the light of dawn,
Is brighter than the gloom of his old grief.
The change was like lightning, blinding and brief;
Secured in the fold where all are as one;
His days of doubts and questioning are done,
Moored safely in the harbor of belief.

He claims to see more clearly than before
He found the light; but there is something blind
In him that once could see an open door
To friends he doesn't visit anymore,
And his own forgotten faces lost behind
The fire in his eyes that once were kind.

Following the Prophet

Years ago I swore I knew God's fire,
Hearing words born beyond the farthest star,
Seeing eyes like Isaiah's gaze in mine,
Feeling sheer exultation rise from a man.

Life was an awesome, tingling, joyous nerve,
Bright with waiting for God's Kingdom to arrive.
Earth, in a flash, would to spirit return,
And I and the faithful in God's eye shine.

I left my life to follow this one man,
More aroused by him than ever again.
Wild with expectancy, we were glad
To forego earth for the treasure ahead.

And yet, he's come and gone and we are here,
Unsaved and seeking, desperate as before.
The Kingdom of all bliss is still unseen;
And I, having merged in faith, am more alone.

Whether deceit or hopeful faith gone bad,
I never knew, and still cannot decide.
There's nothing like the certainty of sham;
Things measure best against the turn of time.

And yet, and yet, I still cannot let go.
What flamed within me then I cannot say,
But I was alive, and for once unalone.
Bravely I rode and in faith was I slain.

And Still We Sing

And Your word
Broke their sword
When our own strength failed us.
                — Rock of Ages

This is the wish forever unfulfilled:
To find in spirit strength to conquer steel;
As if a prophet's flesh could not be killed;
Or power grew in goodness like a shield.

If wanting peace could make the weapons fade,
Or being pure could keep us ever strong;
If love could break the dangerous blade,
Then surely there'd be reason for our song.

But the virtuous fall amid their prayer –
Not faith, nor worth, nor love can change their fate.
Even God, perhaps, winces in despair,
As innocence is stung by the strength of hate.

And still we sing, with hope if not belief,
And still we love, and sing amid our grief.

The Lion and the Ox

One Law for the Lion & Ox is Oppression.
— William Blake

"I blast the bastard soldier
 Who writhes in righteous agony;
 Death to the threatening enemy,
 And I commit no sin."

"Weaponless in the war I sit,
 Accept the peerless death of peace,
 Bleed my blood in deepest love,
 And I commit no sin."

"I sing to my wise and smiling child
 Who lives for joy and nothing more,
 No protest and no fighting for,
 And I commit no sin."

Incantation

Open holy, holy door,
For I, the incarnation, call;
Falling, to rise forevermore,
Or rising till the final fall.

Open holy, holy door,
No more deny the promised throne;
Alone the will can never soar,
Born with spirit bound in bone.

Open unto me the peace,
Ease back the curtains at the core,
Restore the freedom and release
The keys that hold this holy door.

Open unto me the light,
Let night no longer blind my eyes;
Arise, arise, within my sight,
Brightest beauty, bold and wise.

She is of the Sunshine

She is of the sunshine,
Who walks abroad at noon,
And bares her skin to breathe the light,
Close her eyes to world and thought
And lose herself in sun.

I am of the shadow,
The dim, the shaded place.
My eyes are widest in the dark,
Search for all the shapes that lurk,
And dream a paradise.

She from the sun is shaded brown,
And I from the shade am white.
She, in brightness, knows the dark;
I, in dimness, see the light.

She goes forth to find her peace,
I sit still to make my flight.
I stay to seek, she seeks to lose,
And somewhere beyond day and night
Where worlds unfold, we there embrace.

Light all pure can make one blind;
Darkness pure deprives of sight.
We are the realms we leave behind
To change, return, and then to find
We become both dark and bright.

The Bone-Flute

In this cave, a secret place,
The dry remains of sacrifice:
Bones of lamb and crystal beads
Surround the rudely sculpted heads
Of gods or men or demons seen
In this dry cave away from rain,
Where men enacted sacraments
Of foreign and forgotten sense.

Torch-light makes the shadows leap
In this place of man's escape.
The bones are stained with ash and blood,
Stripped of all that once was food:
The hooves that ran too slow to live,
The carcass that they could not save,
And centered in the ritual
The sightless and unspeaking skull.

I pluck a bone from out the dust
And hold it in my bony fist,
And close my eyes. Then, in a stream,
Remove the marks of blood and flame.
I blow into the hollow bone
As if to summon what is gone:
A sudden wail, terror-struck,
A raspy, harsh, and horrid shriek.

There was no meaning in the sound
Blown aloud with breath and bone,
Except that I had given voice
To a once unwilling sacrifice:
Trapped and panicked, breathing stifled,
Agony, confused and wild;
Until the stroke that laid to rest
The stubborn and resisting beast.

Breath had merged my straining throat
With the fleshless relic, ages mute,
And found fulfillment in the note
That made this silent bone a flute.

Egret

Master of movement and master of poise:
The hugeness of wings like waves of white,
The slow, unruffled, majestic rise,
The motion of wings, the motion of light.

Or marble-still in the shadow of trees,
Energy held in a delicate curve,
A painting of grace in a timeless pose,
The fragile rest of a sensitive nerve.

Fly, and this flesh turns to motionless stone,
While the wings of my rising soul release;
Stand, and I move to approach the unknown,
As spirit enfolds to a wingless peace.

A-rise or at rest, the spirit's delight:
The beauty of stillness, the beauty of flight.

A Fierce Warrior in a Suburban Backyard

Youth was a time of building and of play,
Rituals of escaping to our forts.
I once built a passage back to savagery
By the forsythia bush and corner fence.
Using logs and sticks I made a frame,
And piled the rising roof high with leaves.
Though begun in clear daylight as a game,
Night spreads the limits of what one believes.
The wigwam's small door was dark like a cave;
I stared at the primitive hut in fear,
Afraid that a powerful warrior brave
Was waiting inside with a sharpened spear.
The pleasure of the work had made it play,
But entering was better left for day.

Henry

Henry's strong point never was his virtue.
His nastiness and lack of trust could make
A mess of friendships. And we never knew
If what he said were true, or a mistake
Of his imagination, or a lie
Told playfully. But in his absence now,
Missing the way his wild thoughts would fly,
His laughter and his crazy wit, somehow
The quietness disturbs, and his return
Will mean reunion, not confrontation,
And once more we will see if we can live
Together, though there's much for us to learn.
Laughter may yet lead us to salvation.
I'm finding out how much I can forgive.

Drawing a Line

Look, I never easily leave a friend,
But attacking me was his choice, not mine.
I no longer wish to forgive or amend –
Hurt far too often, I now draw the line.
I am glad to be done, to let him go,
Though angered by the mad abuse he used
To cast me out. Looking back, I don't know
Why I stayed so long. I had nothing to lose
By leaving, but a strange friend filled with rage
And tenderness – laughter, cruelty, and pain.
I leave him still locked in his bitter cage,
Loyalty killed by figments in his brain.
What troubles me is how to draw a line
Between sheer meanness and a disturbed mind.

Winter Ways

The chickadee flits from twig to stick
In little leaps of flight.
The robin flies a thousand miles
To miss the cold and ice.

Great strength it takes to fly so far,
And great endurance, too.
But what shall we say of those who stay
And make the most of snow?

A Bird Out of Place

I was cleaning the kitchen window
When a catbird flew inside.
This shy and secret creature
Who loves to sing and hide,
Panicked like a maniac;
I ducked down afraid.
I feared the fierce confusion
Of this desperate singing thing:
Pictured the frantic shrieking beak
Pierce my eye and make me bleed –
As frightened in my feeling
As he was in being trapped
By four walls and a ceiling.
Something in the world was wrong;
Something was where it doesn't belong.
The mirror met his head head-on,
He dropped and fluttered weakly,
Then lay still and sprawled.
I went over meekly,
And buried him back deep in the yard.
Worse than a feeling of grief
Was realizing how hard it was
To feel more than my relief.

Injured Hawk

I first saw you struggling to walk,
Surrounded by creatures
That dared not move too close,
Sensing the ready power
Of talons and beak.
But somehow I came near,
Wrapped you in my coat,
Raised your flinching body,
And gazed into your eyes.
Your eyes: meeting the strange scene
With fierce and outward fearlessness.
I carry that glance within me now,
Of power withheld and voiceless terror,
Forced to trust an awkward creature,
Earth-bound and trembling,
Seeing again and again
How I cupped your body in my hands,
And knew the rigid anxiousness
Of surrendering to another's touch.

The Encounter

The path led to a waterfall and pool,
And there I sat amid the sound and mist,
And looked at the wilder pathless shore
Across the threshold of the water.
Out of the woods came a strong young doe
With her tail in the mouth of an old blind buck
Who followed as if on a string.
She led him to the water till his feet
Felt the cold, and he bent down to drink.
Then the doe saw me – she snorted, then froze;
The old buck grabbed her tail, and waited.
Something in the moment's strangeness
Called to me, and I, too, entered the pool,
Inching my slow way closer and closer,
As the doe snorted and tossed her head,
Shifting her legs, anxious to be gone.
Feeling my own heart's wild rush,
I walked closer; her eyes were locked on me.
She trembled with an agony contained
By loyalty or love; she would not run.
Slowly, I reached my fingers to her fur,
And touched – she flinched, and I pulled back.
The old buck, immense, stood quietly,
And let me lay my hand upon his side
To stroke the fading color of his fur,
As little tingles trickled down my spine.
I laughed within my heart as there we stood,
Locked in the mystery of love and fear.
One and one had met, to travel no longer as two,
And came upon another in his solitude,
Who, knowing a moment of enchantment,
Would walk away and never be the same.

On Finding a Hunting Knife in a Bird Sanctuary

Drawn by the cold blade, I touched it to warm
Flesh; my curious fingers closing firm
To hold the weapon hated by my soul,
And picture in my mind how I could kill.

In self-defense, of course – aroused to rage
By brute attack – a hero's privilege
To strike with innocence, and innocence save;
Right violence allowing virtue to live.

I carried the knife as if ready to kill,
Made bold and daring by a piece of steel;
Feeling safe – till uneasiness crept in,
Having entered a world that feels unclean.

Walking back, I put the knife where it was,
Left in nature where I hope it decays.
Perhaps the day will come for knife or gun,
But I resist the risk of playing Cain.

Atrocities

¶ Based on a dream of Arthur Koestler's

Out of the forest, onto the road,
A wild man, dripping blood –
He seized my arm and tried to speak,
Raving like a lunatic:

Murder, hunger, death, and war –
Dismembered bodies burned in fire –
Headless men – women taken –
Children with their bodies broken –

"Save us! Save us! While you can!
They are killing everyone!"
He tried to pull me off the road
Into the darkness of the wood.

I struggled with the crazy man –
I broke away, and then I ran.

To Mother and Father

Your lives were not the lives that you would choose,
If choice of circumstance were yours to make.
And though shadowed by ancestral sorrows,
You sought again the sun, and chose, with faith
In love, a new beginning in your youth,
Making a promise that age cannot break –
To bear the thorns as you embrace the rose.

I cannot say enough to state my praise,
Or articulate my luckiness of birth.
I know you've had your dark days on this earth;
I know the difficulty of my ways.
Yet, knowing this, my hopes for you are few –
That love has led you faithfully and true,
That joy has not been absent all your days.

TRAVELED

LANDSCAPES

A Rain in Winter

He speaks of diction and imagery
In a classroom of warped-wood floors.
Outside the tall, round-topped windows,
Intermittent waves of wind
Gust and whine with quick pellets
Sounding sharp on hard glass panes.
The surrounding gray vagueness;
The bright, warm room and lecture;
A sad whistle from the window
As if dying in the storm.
The surviving, gray-crusted snow
By the shadowed north corners of buildings
Is diminishing in warm January rain.
Before the rain will bring again
New England flowers, another snow
Will prevail upon the landscape,
A sharper beauty than this uncertainty
Of changing winds and sudden weather.
A starling, swerving in forceful winds
Over brown hills of barren trees
Looks desperate. Inside, though on
The verge of listening and of flight,
No restlessness disturbs my peace
Of willingly going nowhere:
I will know when to move outside.

Waiting for the Whiteness of Spring

Fate, luck, or a wrong turn on a back road
Brought us there. We went to the orchards
With hopes of apple blossoms, tufts of white
In row on row across the sloping hills.
But spring was two weeks behind our eagerness.
Winter held the land as lines of naked claws.
Having found no trees of tender, blooming snow,
No whiteness opening out of branch and bud,
We drove on, not knowing our way too well,
And made a turn onto a shaded road
Through woods of pine, and came upon a home
With a yard of chickens and geese, goats and sheep.
And there, perched on a fence-post by the road,
Was, like a fugitive from a fairy tale,
Or, the spirit of spring, a white peacock.

Neighbors

¶ A response, with all due respect, to Robert Frost's "Mending Wall"

"Good fences make good neighbors," I tell him,
And he's always kind enough to oblige
And meet with me to keep our boundaries clear.
I can tell, though, he thinks it strange of me.
But let the wall fall, and the fields and trees
Run undivided, and grow, and mingle,
Till no man knows his own – then he will see.
And I like my meadow, for though I have
No cows to graze, time was I had many,
And the pasture's still my pleasure to walk
At dawn, with the sun rising and rabbits hiding.
Call it custom, or preference, what you will.
I sometimes think of myself as the pines,
Green in sun or snow, season to season;
Not like his trees that shed their leaves and fruit
Each fall, and each spring start it all again.
I've seen more seasons than I remember,
And many changes, and have learned at times
The dangers of setting things free to grow
That have no sense when left to themselves. No –
I will die here with my pines and pasture,
Even as my father and his before, and preserve
The quiet order for those who are to come.

The Forest

The forest we walked was no sculptured park.
The path was made as much by deer as men.
Peeling birches, mushrooms sprouting out of dark
Stumps, weed clumps, rocks, and here and there a pine
With half its branches dead. The ground was all
Brown leaves losing their form as leaves, soon
To be soil. Rich chaos and decay, the full
Randomness of dead leaves left where they fall.

Chaos to the eye it seemed, yet the mind
Knows how patterns exist in flower, tree,
And leaf; how cells and atoms are designed;
How the whole earth is one enormous sea
Of patterns, inseparable; how one cause
Belongs to a vast, locked world; how this sea
Itself lives by the nature of the laws
That control the place where a dead leaf falls.

Many trees had fallen to the forest floor,
Half-rotted. Such a mad tangle of branch
And bush, trunks at angles slanted, thorns that tore
My coat and skin, drawing blood; then a quick flinch,
Twisting my ankle on the crumbling wood
Of what used to be a tree. Fallen in a trench,
Heavy with sweat and frustration, I was not thrilled
With what I had tasted of the untamed world.

Spotting a lake, we left the trail behind,
Looking forward to a cool, soothing swim.
Only halfway there and you changed your mind,
Tired of fighting a jungle. The game
Of hiking had long since ceased to be fun,
But to return would be as bad as the way we came,
And wanting some relief we struggled on.
I wouldn't admit that the jungle had won.

We reached what should have been a welcome shore,
But all the beauty there we did not see.
Midday. Soundless. Like a silence in war,
The stillness poised. Nothing moved: not a tree,
Not a bird, not a ripple on the lake.
The sun hung hot, the air seemed thick; a bee
Buzzed close, then was gone. Eerie. Nothing to break
The spell. We stood there and looked. Desolate.

Desolate in beauty, but it was not
A beauty for us then. Alien it stood,
An unknown, foreign thing, a world apart:
The sloping flow of forest, a blue lake amid
Green hills. And there we were and wondered why.
What had we to do with this, with a world
We did not know? Far off in the sky
A hawk soared, circling upward out of sight.

The driftwood piled on the shore was thick,
Stretching ten feet into the lake. To swim
Meant stepping on rotting logs, and one slip
Would land a foot in dank and stagnant slime.
A snake slid over a stump and was gone.
"No swimming today," I said with a grim
Smile. We turned on our log and then jumped down,
But it was not solid earth we landed on.

A thick black muck oozed up over our boots,
It grasped our soles and seemed to suck us down,
Pulling us into earth, dragging trapped beasts
Back to a world they thought they had foregone:
To mud and senseless matter. And I heard
Inside my head, that well-embellished bone,
"Return, surrender, and decay." Terrified
Of sudden death, I leapt out of the mud.

With the terror of that strange moment gone,
I turned to see my footprints in the slime.
Brown water filled them, they did not last long,
But the voice in the skull is not so kind.
My mind was occupied with thoughts of mud,
With dying things, the body's slow decline.
I sucked at my scratches and thought of blood,
And how we survive by a tenuous thread.

I saw I was ordered even as a leaf,
That matter formed us both and we formed mud,
So I must belong. That was no relief,
For I did not feel as I thought I should,
For I sought a kinship of the spirit,
Not equivalence with soil. You pulled
A daisy to show me beauty rooted in dirt,
But I was not at peace with nature's art.

The hike back to the cabin was no game;
The morning's search for moose was playful, but no more.
This was a journey long and hard. The strain
Wore away our humor and muscles were sore.
Whatever game I thought there was to win,
I had long ago stopped keeping score;
I conceded to nature, and now begin
To know the laws of the world I live within.

And I thought again of patterns in leaves,
And differences; how every rose is a rose,
But no two alike. Such order weaves
Through matter, such laws, and yet no one knows
The law-maker. Suddenly you looked ahead
And pointed. There was a huge moose, so close
We saw the eyes in his enormous head
Shifting, till he saw us, and then he fled.

I met all existence in that one day,
The mysteries to which I must return,
In thought, at least, until I find a way
To be at home, to walk calmly in the stern
Woods, where I panicked, struck like a snagged deer,
Caught in the fatal trap where I was born:
Forced to confront what is always near,
But desperately hidden, deep with my fear.

The Quarry

There was an old quarry, no longer used,
And an old crane stood like a dinosaur,
Huge, hulking body with a long neck raised
Up, tipped with teeth of steel. The mouth no more
Would clench dense earth, as no more that great brood
Of giants will march their bulk by the shore
Of the lake. And as I stood I wondered:

"But was this a lake long ages ago?
This place where I stand did not stand here then.
This point in space must always exist, though
Deep under rock or deep in the ocean,
I cannot say. And can anyone tell
How many places this one place has been,
And will become, when I have long been still?"

We tried to guess the story of each age,
Each clear layer of the long colored stone,
Shaded gray or brown; an eon – one short stage
In an on-going world. How much wood and bone
To make an inch of earth? That layer like rust –
Ten thousand years of trees, perhaps; all gone.
A thriving forest cast to hard, dry crust.

We looked at each other, then at the cliff,
That towering wall, and I saw the earth
As that round rock you picked and hurled, as if
To put in orbit, and wondered what worth
I could find in this world; again I gazed
At you, and something stirred as if in birth,
And where there's birth, there's something to be praised.

The Orchard

Autumn was old, the harvest was all done.
Countless constellations of apples – red,
Green and golden, had long been picked and gone.
"Try a free sip of cider," the farmer said.
We did, and asked if we could walk around.
The owner of the apples nodded his head,
"But the only apples are on the ground."

Apples always turn my thoughts to Eden,
To the senseless order – the law that brought pain
To paradise. I, being a heathen,
Dismiss Father and Devil with disdain,
And search to find for me a worthy God;
Not easy, given the nature of my brain:
I'd leave a church to breathe in goldenrod.

No God's garden there, no oasis lush
Like Eden bursting forth with boundless green,
But each tree planned and planted without rush,
Elegantly ordered, composed, serene.
"Like lines of soldiers," I said with dismay,
"Or else assembly parts to some machine."
"No. I see lines of dancers in a play."

The linear beauty was simple and strict;
Nothing original and nothing left to guess.
As sure as the fact that all apples were picked
And sent to market, or the cider-press.
The landscape was a pattern, a truth it seems,
For me to ridicule and you to bless,
As we argued it onward to extremes.

We slanted through rows to avoid routine;
I refused to stroll the aisles one by one.
The rows were the farmer's and I didn't mean
To follow in footsteps so frequently done.
Our walk was unpredictable, each turn
An unconsidered choosing come and gone
Unguessed, our pathlessness of no concern.

What happened next was a nice stroke of luck,
And though not searching, we certainly did find.
You, the actor, like a holy man star-struck
With wonder, touched the golden fruit with blind
Adoration: "A gift from God, a miracle!"
Amused, but hungry, I said, "If you don't mind,
Let's eat the damn thing, it's only an apple."

"I bless this golden fruit, I touch the sun,
Here embodied in this essence of light."
You lifted gently and it came undone,
As if it had let go, as if it might
Have dropped the very second you held your hand
To pick it, and somehow at just the right
Moment we wandered along as if planned.

You said a sort of Grace, and with a grin
Opened wide and took a loud crunching bite,
Chewing the honey-like sweetness held within,
Then laughing fell down backwards with delight.
You decided to be a friend and share,
And I too ate eagerly of the white
Flesh, and something changed within me there.

The cold was crisp and the grass more than green;
The sun on my skin was a touch I could feel.
Such joy in your face I never had seen;
Suddenly things were more dream-like than real:
How we ran down the hill, weaving through trees,
Like beings perfected with no more to heal,
Till reaching the barn we dropped to our knees.

My friend, you were there, in you I can trust.
We don't know what happened, but know it's true.
No Eden, no angels, no serpent – just
An apple overlooked by the local crew.
We walked out past the pigsty, where hogs chew
The cider-pressings given them to eat.
We somehow had tasted sacredness, and it was sweet.

The Mountain

"A hell of a honeymoon," I said at last.
Five hours up over trails of loose rock,
With every tired step a threat to twist
An ankle or knee. We reached the peak
And walked amid the clouds without a guide,
Though all we had wanted was a scenic trail.
This long, hard climbing caught us unprepared –
Passing the tree-line where all forests fail,
Left without covering, open to the sun,
Naked to danger and strangely alone.

I looked around and saw little but mist,
Except below and three thousand feet down,
A lake. But that was far away and first
We had to walk the razor's edge – a spine
Of rock with sides that dropped a half-mile.
We were committed, that was clear; no way
To wish ourselves home, or wake with a smile
From a dream. No, we were up there to stay
Until we chose to return or go on,
Left to ourselves with the sun going down.

"You shall be for each other – legs and eyes:
To see far more than one alone can see,
To watch and respond, to learn and be wise,
To carry when needed, and then to set free."
The rabbi spoke well, but where was he now?
What words for a couple learning to climb?
"Balance the sight and the strength, and allow
Yourselves each to be carried when such time
Comes, and times will change. The one who can must
Lead, but in turn will follow. And have trust."

The mountain stripped nature to the bone.
Trees were gone; not even weeds could survive
On the ground where we stood. Nothing but stone
And sky, and the cold wind. Nothing alive
But us. I gazed into the swirling cloud,
Like Moses on Sinai, lost in a storm,
And thought, "Hear, O Israel, the Lord our God,
The Lord is One." Are these words the form
For a deathless moment, wild and stern,
Stunned by a force eternally reborn?

Moses climbed a mountain, journeyed on stone
To meet with that whose nature, like a soul,
Cannot be held; and to name an unknown
Is not to know or even to reveal,
But only diminish to fit a word.
"Spirit," I said as the sun went down red.
Why does barren rock – heavy, cold, and hard –
Stir thoughts of spirit? And what's left unsaid,
Having pronounced the letters and made a sound,
When words cannot carry the worlds we intend?

We kissed; the feel of living flesh was sweet;
Something other than wind, stone, sky, or sun;
Other than words or spirit; more complete,
Perhaps, than any element alone.
And frailer, too. On a precarious ridge
We sat, scared of the difficult trail we came,
Scared more of the sinister razor-edge,
And wanting only to be safely home.
The mountain wind seemed strong enough to throw
Us off the edge. You stood and said, "Let's go."

I rose to take whatever path you meant,
When an older couple came into view.
I asked about the razor; they said, "Don't.
Some today have done it, but just a few;
The wind is wild." "We want to get down
The shortest way." "Then follow us," they said,
"It's short, but steep." And quickly they had gone
Over the edge and out of sight. Not dead,
For I could see their heads bobbing below,
Moving from rock to rock, and easily so.

Slowly, down on all fours, I took the lead,
Hugging the rock against the raging wind.
I dared not move quickly, but wished for speed.
Groping for footholds, reaching my feet blind
Into space, dangling till I found a rock
To stand on; pointing where to put your feet.
"Doing fine," I said as I held your back
And you dropped to where I stood. "Getting late,"
I thought. Then a rock slipped and I nearly fell.
I scrambled for holds and stifled a yell.

That shook me; every step was now a trial,
Testing stones, sliding slowly down from hold
To hold, following your lead, your smile
Always encouraging in the dim, cold
Air. I pictured you falling from the cliff,
And saving you. And then your saving me.
I pictured both of us falling – what if
It happened? Such things do happen. Each knee
Hurt, my arms and legs were shaking from the strain.
My voice quivered, too, but from fear, not pain.

I took hold of a skinny trunk of pine –
Trees! Reaching the trees was like coming home
And crawling under a blanket. "Doing fine."
Safe, with branches to hold and shelter from
The wind. The lake was close now. So much fear
Of falling, and agony of being left
If you had fallen. And all I could hear
Were the words we had spoken as a pledge,
Grown beyond words to a life of their own
In the joyous risk of devotion to one.

Our last steps down the hill were in the dark,
Leaping along the path, bouncing from stone
To stone; somehow my body seemed to work
Its best, released from fear, trusting its own
Sense. I did not know how capable it was –
How capable I was, I guess I should say.
Alive with new spirit, I felt no flaws,
No soreness or doubts – a child at play.
Running hand in hand we splashed in the lake,
Laughed at its coldness, all senses awake.

We had passed through clouds and over cold stone
To stand again on the wide, stable earth.
"You shall be as two trees that intertwine,
Two spirits eternally giving birth."
Ah, spirit and stone. Perhaps both endure.
Did Moses give his vision form as laws?
Is flesh the shape that spirit takes? Not sure
Of that – who is the God whom Moses calls?
God is one, perhaps as you and I are one,
Beyond all words, united and alone.

The Forest Through the Night

The scent of evergreens from our fire
Traveled far upon the air. The evening
Brought forth life as we walked in growing dark.
Salamanders – bright orange – on a mat
Of oak leaves, dry and brown; their tiny limbs –
Like infants crawling in an unknown world –
Delicate skin on bodies soft and small –
Scurrying with fear at the giant force
That hauled them off the earth – hands that lifted
And placed them home. A sudden plunge – a beaver's
Loud announcement of our threatening presence;
Comforted by our silence and withdrawal,
He returns to much the bark of a twig.
The strange, raspy snort of a startled deer,
Protesting or warning of our coming,
Who runs, stops, and turns to watch intruders;
Hears whispers, and walks off into darkness.
We passed a nest of broken turtle eggs,
Cracked and curled and still dripping wet with birth.
We headed back and settled in our camp.

An owl, far away, filled the woods with sound.
What is spoken in those calls, and to whom?
How is a mate ever found in the dark,
But by number and rhythm of coos and calls?
For how many ages have great horned owls
Chanted the same resounding notes?
Does anyone change the communal song
And listen in the stillness for response?
So we talked around our smoky fire,
Filled with the rich smell of charcoal and pine;
Four friends telling stories and reciting
Poems; voices rising out of darkness,
Words arising out of age and distance
To speak again across the centuries
And be heard. We spoke until tiredness
Spread us into pairs, and sent us to sleep.
I woke and listened to a calling owl,

Singing for a mate, or just for the sound.
We lay together, warm with sleep, and then,
Naked in the stillness of night, embraced.

We woke while the sky was starry and black,
And walked to a lake we could not yet see.
I realized how little I look at stars.
I closed my eyes and felt the forceful wind
Lift my hair, rushing loudly in my ears.
The wind like the breathing of vastness blew,
Raising white waves on the water below.
It had begun. Across the void a line
Appeared where light and dark divided space,
And mountain and sky were two, not one. Then,
Over the water there rose a cold mist,
The alien breath of a world's new birth,
As the sun cast the earth into color:
The gray of water, the green of the trees,
The delicate, yellow-white glow of dawn.
We witnessed creation without a word;
The working of this wide, revolving world.
Returning to sleep, I thought of the sun –
And of owls – and the far, forgotten stars –
Known through a night in the forest till dawn.

Snow-Play

That was the last day we were together,
A strange day of hiking through knee-deep snow
To stand by the edge of a frozen lake
And gaze at where it disappeared in white,
Somewhere in the distance. Two friends and I,
Three notes united in a chord that used
To play abundantly, struck once again.

Down on our knees, rolling boulders of snow,
Heaving, grunting, laughing – alive and lost
In whiteness. With a boulder from each
We made a man; then, rolled the snow again,
Till three great orbs formed a line to the lake,
And standing on our pedestals of snow,
Screamed – and heard our voices sound through the hills.

The noise of our cries just echoed and died;
The sculptures, melting, could be seen for months –
Dwindling monuments to that one hour
In snow, when time was deep and we were free
In ways I seldom know and cannot say.
Now the miles keep us from communing.
I wait for the day we return to play.

Peter Langman was founder and editor of *The Rose's Hope,* a literary journal that published from 1979 through 1984. During its brief tenure, the journal was nominated for the Poetry Fifty as one of the top fifty poetry markets in the country. He is currently editor-in-chief of the *Lehigh Valley Literary Review.* His poems have appeared in *Crosscurrents: A Quarterly, Blue Unicorn, Negative Capability, Spirit, Candelabrum, Unabridged,* and others. Langman is also a playwright whose scripts have received recognition in national competitions. His plays have had readings and performances in Pennsylvania and New York. Two monologues ("Anorexia" and "Obesity Talks Back") from his play "Hunger" appear in *Young Women's Monologues from Contemporary Plays, #2.* Langman is a psychologist and author of the books *Jewish Issues in Multiculturalism* and *Why Kids Kill: Inside the Minds of School Shooters.*

www.ingramcontent.com/pod-product-compliance
Lightning Source LLC
Chambersburg PA
CBHW020904090426
42736CB00008B/492